DEPARTMENTAL DITTIES

Departmental Ditties and Ballads and Barrack Room Ballads

By Rudyard Kipling

PUBLISHED BY
DOUBLEDAY, PAGE & COMPANY

FOR
REVIEW OF REVIEWS CO.
1915

CONTENTS

DEPARTMENTAL DITTIES

OTHER VERSES

BARRACK-ROOM BALLADS

PRELUDE

I have eaten your bread and salt,
  I have drunk your water and wine;
The deaths ye died I have watched beside,
  And the lives that ye led were mine.

Was there aught that I did not share
  In vigil or toil or ease,—
One joy or woe that I did not know,
  Dear hearts across the seas?

I have written the tale of our life
  For a sheltered people's mirth,
In jesting guise — but ye are wise,
  And ye know what the jest is worth.

DEPARTMENTAL DITTIES

GENERAL SUMMARY

WE are very slightly changed
From the semi-apes who ranged
   India's prehistoric clay;
Whoso drew the longest bow
Ran his brother down, you know,
   As we run men down to-day.

"Dowb," the first of all his race,
Met the Mammoth face to face
   On the lake or in the cave,
Stole the steadiest canoe,
Ate the quarry others slew,
   Died — and took the finest grave.

When they scratched the reindeer-bone,
Some one made the sketch his own,
   Filched it from the artist — then,
Even in those early days,
Won a simple Viceroy's praise
   Through the toil of other men.

Ere they hewed the Sphinx's visage
Favouritism governed kissage,
Even as it does in this age.

Who shall doubt the secret hid
Under Cheops' pyramid
Was that the contractor did
   Cheops out of several millions?
Or that Joseph's sudden rise
To Comptroller of Supplies
Was a fraud of monstrous size
   On King Pharaoh's swart Civilian?

Thus, the artless songs I sing
Do not deal with anything
   New or never said before.
As it was in the beginning
Is to-day official sinning,
   And shall be for evermore.

ARMY HEAD-QUARTERS

Old is the song that I sing —
Old as my unpaid bills —
Old as the chicken that kitmutgars *bring*
Men at dâk-bungalows — old as the Hills.

AHASUERUS JENKINS of the "Operatic Own,"
Was dowered with a tenor voice of *super*-Santley tone.
His views on equitation were, perhaps, a trifle queer;
He had no seat worth mentioning, but oh! he had an
ear.

He clubbed his wretched company a dozen times a
day,
He used to leave his charger in a parabolic way,
His method of saluting was the joy of all beholders,
But Ahasuerus Jenkins had a head upon his shoulders.

He took two months at Simla when the year was
at the spring.
And underneath the deodars eternally did sing.

13

He warbled like a *bul-bul*, but particularly at
Cornelia Agrippina, who was musical and fat.

She controlled a humble husband, who, in turn,
    controlled a Dept.,
Where Cornelia Agrippina's human singing-birds
    were kept
From April to October on a plump retaining fee,
Supplied, of course, *per mensem*, by the Indian
    Treasury.

Cornelia used to sing to him, and Jenkins used to
    play;
He praised unblushingly her notes, for he was false
    as they;
So when the winds of April turned the budding roses
    brown,
Cornelia told her husband:— Tom, you mustn't
    send him down.

They haled him from his regiment, which didn't
    much regret him;
They found for him an office-stool, and on that stool
    they set him.

To play with maps and catalogues three idle hours a
     day,
And draw his plump retaining fee — which means
     his double pay.

Now, ever after dinner, when the coffee-cups are
     brought,
Ahasuerus waileth o'er the grand pianoforte;
And, thanks to fair Cornelia, his fame hath waxen
     great,
And Ahasuerus Jenkins is a power in the State!

STUDY OF AN ELEVATION, IN INDIAN INK

This ditty is a string of lies.
But — how the deuce did Gubbins rise?

POTIPHAR GUBBINS, C. E.,
Stands at the top of the tree;
And I muse in my bed on the reasons that led
To the hoisting of Potiphar G.

Potiphar Gubbins, C. E.,
Is seven years junior to Me;
Each bridge that he makes either buckles or breaks,
And his work is as rough as he.

Potiphar Gubbins, C. E.,
Is coarse as a chimpanzee;
And I can't understand why you gave him your hand,
Lovely Mehitabel Lee.

Potiphar Gubbins, C. E.,
Is dear to the Powers that Be;

For They bow and They smile in an affable style,
   Which is seldom accorded to Me.

   Potiphar Gubbins, C. E.,
   Is certain as certain can be
Of a highly paid post which is claimed by a host
   Of seniors — including Me.

   Careless and lazy is he,
   Greatly inferior to Me.
What is the spell that you manage so well,
   Commonplace Potiphar G.?

   Lovely Mehitabel Lee,
   Let me inquire of thee,
Should I have riz to where Potiphar is
   Hadst thou been mated to Me?

DELILAH

We have another Viceroy now, those days are dead
and done
Of Delilah Aberyswith and depraved Ulysses Gunne.

DELILAH ABERYSWITH was a lady — not too young—
With a perfect taste in dresses and a badly bitted
tongue,
With a thirst for information, and a greater thirst
for praise,
And a little house in Simla in the Prehistoric Days.

By reason of her marriage to a gentleman in power,
Delilah was acquainted with the gossip of the hour;
And many little secrets, of a half-official kind,
Were whispered to Delilah, and she bore them all in
mind.

She patronized extensively a man, Ulysses Gunne,
Whose mode of earning money was a low and shame-
ful one.

18

He wrote for divers papers, which, as everybody
    knows,
Is worse than serving in a shop or scaring off the
    crows.

He praised her queenly beauty first; and, later on, he
    hinted
At the vastness of her intellect with compliment
    unstinted;
He went with her a-riding, and his love for her was
    such
That he lent her all his horses and — she galled them
    very much.

One day THEY brewed a secret of a fine financial
    sort;
It related to Appointments, to a Man and a Report.
'Twas almost worth the keeping [only seven people
    knew it],
So Gunne rose up to seek the truth and patiently
    ensue it.

It was a Viceroy's Secret, but — perhaps the wine
    was red —
Perhaps an Aged Councillor had lost his aged head —

Perhaps Delilah's eyes were bright — Delilah's whispers sweet —

The Aged Member told her what 'twere treason to
repeat.

Ulysses went a-riding, and they talked of love and
flowers;

Ulysses went a-calling, and he called for several
hours;

Ulysses went a-waltzing, and Delilah helped him
dance —

Ulysses let the waltzes go, and waited for his chance.

The summer sun was setting, and the summer air was
still,

The couple went a-walking in the shade of Summer
Hill,

The wasteful sunset faded out in turkis-green and
gold,

Ulysses pleaded softly, and . . . that bad Delilah
told!

Next morn, a startled Empire learnt the all-impor-
tant News;

Next week, the Aged Councillor was shaking in his
shoes;

Next month, I met Delilah, and she did not show the least

Hesitation in asserting that Ulysses was a "beast."

.   .   .   .

We have another Viceroy now, those days are dead and done —

Of Delilah Aberyswith and most mean Ulysses Gunne!

A LEGEND OF THE FOREIGN OFFICE

This is the reason why Rustum Beg,
Rajah of Kolazai,
Drinketh the "simpkin" and brandy peg,
Maketh the money to fly,
Vexeth a Government, tender and kind,
Also — but this is a detail — blind.

RUSTUM BEG of Kolazai — slightly backward Native
State —
Lusted for a C. S. I.— so began to sanitate.
Built a Gaol and Hospital — nearly built a City
drain —
Till his faithful subjects all thought their ruler was
insane.

Strange departures made he then — yea, Depart-
ments stranger still,
Half a dozen Englishmen helped the Rajah with a will,
Talked of noble aims and high, hinted of a future fine
For the State of Kolazai, on a strictly Western line.

Rajah Rustum held his peace; lowered octroi dues
    one half;
Organized a State Police; purified the Civil Staff;
Settled cess and tax afresh in a very liberal way;
Cut temptations of the flesh — also cut the Bukh-
    shi's pay;

Roused his Secretariat to a fine Mahratta fury,
By a Hookum hinting at supervision of *dasturi;*
Turned the state of Kolazai very nearly upside-down;
When the end of May was nigh waited his achieve-
    ment crown.

Then the Birthday honours came.   Sad to state and
    sad to see,
Stood against the Rajah's name nothing more than
    C. I. E.!

.   .   .   .

Things were lively for a week in the State of Kolazai,
Even now the people speak of that time regretfully;

How he disendowed the Gaol — stopped at once the
    City drain;
Turned to beauty fair and frail — got his senses back
    again;

Doubled taxes, cesses all; cleared away each new-
    built *thana;*
Turned the two-lakh Hospital into a superb Zenana;

Heaped upon the Bukhshi Sahib wealth and honours
    manifold;
Clad himself in Eastern garb — squeezed his people
    as of old.
Happy, happy Kolazai! Never more will Rustum
    Beg
Play to catch the Viceroy's eye. He prefers the
    "simpkin" peg.

THE STORY OF URIAH

"Now there were two men in one city; the one rich,
and the other poor."

> JACK BARRETT went to Quetta
>   Because they told him to.
> He left his wife at Simla
>   On three-fourths his monthly screw.
> Jack Barrett died at Quetta
>   Ere the next month's pay he drew.
>
> Jack Barrett went to Quetta,
>   He didn't understand
> The reason of his transfer
>   From the pleasant mountain-land:
> The season was September,
>   And it killed him out of hand.
>
> Jack Barrett went to Quetta
>   And there gave up the ghost;
> Attempting two men's duty
>   In that very healthy post;

And Mrs. Barrett mourned for him
  Five lively months at most.

Jack Barrett's bones at Quetta
  Enjoy profound repose;
But I shouldn't be astonished
  If now his spirit knows
The reason of his transfer
  From the Himalayan snows.

And, when the Last Great Bugle Call
  Adown the Hurnai throbs,
When the last grim joke is entered
  In the big black Book of Jobs,
And Quetta graveyards give again
  Their victims to the air,
I shouldn't like to be the man,
  Who sent Jack Barrett there.

THE POST THAT FITTED

Though tangled and twisted the course of true love,
This ditty explains
No tangle's so tangled it cannot improve
If the Lover has brains.

ERE the steamer bore him Eastward, Sleary was
engaged to marry
An attractive girl at Tunbridge, whom he called
"my little Carrie."
Sleary's pay was very modest; Sleary was the other
way.
Who can cook a two-plate dinner on eight paltry
dibs a day?

Long he pondered o'er the question in his scantly
furnished quarters —
Then proposed to Minnie Boffkin, eldest of Judge
Boffkin's daughters.
Certainly an impecunious Subaltern was not a catch
But the Boffkins knew that Minnie mightn't make
another match.

So they recognized the business and, to feed and
    clothe the bride,
Got him made a Something-Something somewhere
    on the Bombay side.
Anyhow, the billet carried pay enough for him to
    marry —
As the artless Sleary put it:—"Just the thing for me
    and Carrie."

Did he, therefore, jilt Miss Boffkin — impulse of a
    baser mind?
No! He started epileptic fits of an appalling kind.
[Of his *modus operandi* only this much I could
    gather:—
"Pears shaving sticks will give you little taste and
    lots of lather."]

Frequently in public places his affliction used to
    smite
Sleary with distressing vigour — always in the Boff-
    kins' sight.
Ere a week was over Minnie weepingly returned his
    ring,
Told him his "unhappy weakness" stopped all
    thought of marrying.

Sleary bore the information with a chastened holy
 joy,——
[Epileptic fits don't matter in Political employ,]
Wired three short words to Carrie — took his ticket,
 packed his kit —
Bade farewell to Minnie Boffkin in one last, long,
 lingering fit.

Four weeks later, Carrie Sleary read — and laughed
 until she wept —
Mrs. Boffkin's warning letter on the "wretched
 epilept."
Year by year, in pious patience, vengeful Mrs. Boffkin sits
Waiting for the Sleary babies to develop Sleary's fits.

A CODE OF MORALS

Lest you should think this story true
I merely mention I
Evolved it lately.   'Tis a most
Unmitigated misstatement.

Now Jones had left his new-wed bride to keep his
   house in order.
And hied away to the Hurrum Hills above the
   Afghan border,
To sit on a rock with a heliograph; but ere he left
   he taught
His wife the working of the Code that sets the miles
   at naught.

And Love had made him very sage, as Nature made
   her fair;
So Cupid and Apollo linked, *per* heliograph, the pair.
At dawn, across the Hurrum Hills, he flashed her
   counsel wise —
At e'en, the dying sunset bore her husband's
   homilies.

He warned her 'gainst seductive youths in scarlet
    clad and gold,
As much as 'gainst the blandishments paternal of the
    old;
But kept his gravest warnings for (hereby my ditty
    hangs)
That snowy-haired Lothario Lieutenant-General
    Bangs.

'Twas General Bangs, with Aide and Staff, that tit-
    tupped on the way,
When they beheld a heliograph tempestuously at play.
They thought of Border risings, and of stations
    sacked and burnt —
So stopped to take the message down — and this is
    what they learnt:—

"Dash dot dot, dot, dot dash, dot dash dot" twice.
    The General swore.
"Was ever General Officer addressed as 'dear'
    before?
" 'My Love,' i' faith! 'My Duck,' Gadzooks!
    'My darling popsy-wop!'
"Spirit of great Lord Wolseley, *who* is on that
    mountain top?"

The artless Aide-de-camp was mute; the gilded Staff
      were still,
As, dumb with pent-up mirth, they booked that
      message from the hill;
For clear as summer-lightning flare, the husband's
      warning ran:—
"Don't dance or ride with General Bangs — a most
      immoral man."

[At dawn, across the Hurrum Hills, he flashed her
      counsel wise —
But, howsoever Love be blind, the world at large
      hath eyes.]
With damnatory dot and dash he heliographed his
      wife
Some interesting details of the General's private life.

The artless Aide-de-camp was mute; the shining
      Staff were still,
And red and ever redder grew the General's shaven
      gill.
And this is what he said at last (his feelings matter
      not):—
"I think we've tapped a private line. Hi! Threes
      about there! Trot!"

All honour unto Bangs, for ne'er did Jones thereafter
    know
By word or act official who read off that helio;
But the tale is on the Frontier, and from Michni to
    Mool*tan*
They know the worthy General as "that most im-
    moral man."

PUBLIC WASTE

Walpole talks of "a man and his price,"
List to a ditty queer —
The sale of a Deputy-Acting-Vice-
Resident-Engineer
Bought like a bullock, hoof and hide,
By the Little Tin Gods on the Mountain Side.

By the laws of the Family Circle 'tis written in
letters of brass

That only a Colonel from Chatham can manage the
Railways of State,

Because of the gold on his breeks, and the subjects
wherein he must pass;

Because in all matters that deal not with Railways
his knowledge is great.

Now Exeter Battleby Tring had laboured from boy-
hood to eld

On the Lines of the East and the West, likewise of
the North and South;

34

Many lines had he built and surveyed — important
    the posts which he held;
And the Lords of the Iron Horse were dumb when he
    opened his mouth.

Black as the raven his garb, and his heresies jettier
    still —
Hinting that Railways required lifetimes of study
    and knowledge —
Never clanked sword by his side — Vauban he
    knew not, nor drill —
Nor was his name on the list of men who had passed
    through the "College."

Wherefore the Little Tin Gods harried their little
    tin souls,
Seeing he came not from Chatham, jingled no spurs
    at his heels,
Knowing that, nevertheless, was he first on the
    Government rolls
For the billet of "Railway Instructor to Little Tin
    Gods on Wheels."

Letters not seldom they wrote him, "having the
    honour to state,"

It would be better for all men if he were laid on the
        shelf:

Much would accrue to his bank-book and he con-
        sented to wait

Until the Little Tin Gods built him a berth for him-
        self.

"Special, well paid, and exempt from the Law of the
        Fifty and Five,

Even to Ninety and Nine" — these were the terms of
        the pact:

Thus did the Little Tin Gods (long may their High-
        nesses thrive!)

Silence his mouth with rupees, keeping their Circle
        intact;

Appointing a Colonel from Chatham who managed
        the Bhamo State Line,

(The which was one mile and one furlong — a
        guaranteed twenty-inch gauge)

So Exeter Battleby Tring consented his claims to
        resign,

And died, on four thousand a month, in the nine-
        tieth year of his age!

WHAT HAPPENED

HURREE Chunder Mookerjee, pride of Bow Bazar,
Owner of a native press, "Barrishter-at-Lar,"
Waited on the Government with a claim to wear
Sabres by the bucketful, rifles by the pair.

Then the Indian Government winked a wicked wink,
Said to Chunder Mookerjee: "Stick to pen and ink.
They are safer implements, but, if you insist,
We will let you carry arms wheresoe'er you list."

Hurree Chunder Mookerjee sought the gunsmith and
Bought the tubes of Lancaster, Ballard, Dean, and
    Bland,
Bought a shiny bowie-knife, bought a town-made
    sword,
Jingled like a carriage-horse when he went abroad.

But the Indian Government, always keen to please,
Also gave permission to horrid men like these —
Yar Mahommed Yusufzai, down to kill or steal;
Chimbu Singh from Bikaneer, Tantia the Bhil;

Killar Khan the Marri chief, Jowar Singh the Sikh,
Nubbee Baksh Punjabi Jat, Abdul Huq Rafiq —
He was a Wahabi; last, little Boh Hla-oo
Took advantage of the Act — took a Snider too.

They were unenlightened men, Ballard knew them
    not,
They procured their swords and guns chiefly on the
    spot,
And the lore of centuries, plus a hundred fights.
Made them slow to disregard one another's rights.

With a unanimity dear to patriot hearts
All those hairy gentlemen out of foreign parts
Said: "The good old days are back — let us go to
    war!"
Swaggered down the Grand Trunk Road into Bow
    Bazar.

Nubbee Baksh Punjabi Jat found a hide-bound flail,
Chimbu Singh from Bikaneer oiled his Tonk jezail,
Yar Mohammed Yusufzai spat and grinned with glee
As he ground the butcher-knife of the Khyberee.

Jowar Singh the Sikh procured sabre, quoit, and mace,
Abdul Huq, Wahabi, took his dagger from its place,

While amid the jungle-grass danced and grinned and
    jabbered
Little Boh Hla-oo and cleared the dah-blade from
    the scabbard.

What became of Mookerjee? Soothly, who can say?
Yar Mahommed only grins in a nasty way,
Jowar Singh is reticent, Chimbu Singh is mute;
But the belts of all of them simply bulge with loot.

What became of Ballard's guns? Afghans black and
    grubby
Sell them for their silver weight to the men of Pubbi;
And the shiny bowie-knife and the town-made
    sword are
Hanging in a Marri camp just across the Border.

What became of Mookerjee? Ask Mahommed Yar
Prodding Siva's sacred bull down the Bow Bazar.
Speak to placid Nubbee Baksh — question land and
    sea —
Ask the Indian Congress men — only don't ask me!

THE MAN WHO COULD WRITE

Shun — shun the Bowl!   That fatal, facile drink
   Has ruined many geese who dipped their quills in't.
Bribe, murder, marry, but steer clear of Ink
   Save when you write receipts for paid-up bills in't.
There may be silver in the "blue-black"—all
I know of is the iron and the gall.

Boanerges Blitzen, servant of the Queen,
Is a dismal failure — is a Might-have-been.
In a luckless moment he discovered men
Rise to high position through a ready pen.

Boanerges Blitzen argued therefore — "I,
With the selfsame weapon, can attain as high."
Only he did not possess when he made the trial,
Wicked wit of C-lv-n, irony of L — l.

[Men who spar with Government need, to back their
      blows,
Something more than ordinary journalistic prose.]

Never young Civilian's prospects were so bright,
Till an Indian paper found that he could write:
Never young Civilian's prospects were so dark,
When the wretched Blitzen wrote to make his mark.

Certainly he scored it, bold, and black, and firm —
In that Indian paper made his seniors squirm —
Quoted office scandals, wrote the tactless truth —
Was there ever known a more misguided youth?

When the Indian paper praised his plucky game,
Boanerges Blitzen felt that this was fame:
When the men he wrote of shook their heads and
    swore,
Boanerges Blitzen only wrote the more;

Posed as Young Ithuriel, resolute and grim,
Till he found promotion didn't come to him;
Till he found that reprimands weekly were his lot,
And his many Districts curiously hot.

Till he found his furlough strangely hard to win,
Boanerges Blitzen didn't care a pin:
Then it seemed to dawn on him something wasn't
    right —
Boanerges Blitzen put it down to "spite."

Languished in a District desolate and dry;
Watched the Local Government yearly pass him by;
Wondered where the hitch was; called it most unfair.

.   .   .   .

That was seven years ago — and he still is there.

PINK DOMINOES

"They are fools who kiss and tell"—
Wisely has the poet sung.
Man may hold all sorts of posts
If he'll only hold his tongue.

JENNY and Me were engaged, you see
   On the eve of the Fancy Ball;
So a kiss or two was nothing to you
   Or any one else at all.

Jenny would go in a domino —
   Pretty and pink but warm;
While I attended, clad in a splendid
   Austrian uniform.

Now we had arranged, through notes exchanged
   Early that afternoon,
At Number Four to waltz no more,
   But to sit in the dusk and spoon.

[I wish you to see that Jenny and Me
   Had barely exchanged our troth;

So a kiss or two was strictly due
    By, from, and between us both.]

When Three was over, an eager lover,
    I fled to the gloom outside;
And a Domino came out also
    Whom I took for my future bride.

That is to say, in a casual way,
    I slipped my arm around her;
With a kiss or two (which is nothing to you),
    And ready to kiss I found her.

She turned her head and the name she said
    Was certainly not my own;
But ere I could speak, with a smothered shriek
    She fled and left me alone.

Then Jenny came, and I saw with shame,
    She'd doffed her domino;
And I had embraced a stranger's waist —
    But I did not tell her so.

Next morn I knew that there were two
    Dominoes pink, and one

Had cloaked the spouse of Sir Julian Vouse,
  Our big Political gun.

Sir J. was old, and her hair was gold,
  And her eyes were a blue cerulean;
And the name she said when she turned her head
  Was not in the least like "Julian."

Now wasn't it nice, when want of *pice*
  Forbade us twain to marry,
That old Sir J. in the kindest way,
  Made me his Secre*tarry?*

MUNICIPAL

"Why is my District death-rate low?"
Said Binks of Hezabad.
"Wells, drains, and sewage-outfalls are
"My own peculiar fad.
"I learnt a lesson once.   It ran
"Thus," quoth that most veracious man:—

It was an August evening, and in snowy garments
 clad,
I paid a round of visits in the lines of Hezabad;
When, presently, my Waler saw, and did not like
 at all
A Commissariat elephant careering down the Mall.

I couldn't see the driver, and across my mind it rushed
That that Commissariat elephant had suddenly gone
 musth.
I didn't care to meet him, and I couldn't well get
 down,
So I let the Waler have it, and we headed for the
 town.

The buggy was a new one and, praise Dykes, it stood
the strain

Till the Waler jumped a bullock just above the City
Drain;

And the next that I remember was a hurricane of
squeals,

And the creature making toothpicks of my five-foot
patent wheels.

He seemed to want the owner, so I fled, distraught
with fear,

To the Main Drain sewage-outfall where he snorted
in my ear —

Reached the four-foot drain-head safely, and in
darkness and despair,

Felt the brute's proboscis fingering my terror
stiffened hair.

Heard it trumpet on my shoulder — tried to crawl a
little higher —

Found the Main Drain sewage-outfall blocked, some
eight feet up, with mire;

And, for twenty reeking minutes, Sir, my very
marrow froze,

While the trunk was feeling blindly for a purchase on
my toes!

It missed me by a fraction, but my hair was turning
gray
Before they called the drivers up and dragged the
brute away.
Then I sought the City Elders, and my words were
very plain.
They flushed that four-foot drain-head and — it
never choked again.

You may hold with surface-drainage, and the sun-
for garbage cure,
Till you've been a periwinkle shrinking coyly up a
sewer.
I believe in well-flushed culverts. . . .

This is why the death-rate's small;
And, if you don't believe me, get *shikarred* yourself.
That's all.

THE LAST DEPARTMENT

Twelve hundred million men are spread
About this Earth, and I and You
Wonder, when You and I are dead,
What will those luckless millions do?

"NONE whole or clean," we cry, "or free from stain
Of favour."   Wait awhile, till we attain
   The Last Department where nor fraud nor fools,
Nor grade nor greed, shall trouble us again.

Fear, Favour, or Affection — what are these
To the grim Head who claims our services?
   I never knew a wife or interest yet
Delay that *pukka* step, miscalled "decease";

When leave, long over-due, none can deny;
When idleness of all Eternity
   Becomes our furlough, and the marigold
Our thriftless, bullion-minting Treasury

Transferred to the Eternal Settlement,
Each in his strait, wood-scantled office pent,
   No longer Brown reverses Smith's appeals,
Or Jones records his Minute of Dissent.

And One, long since a pillar of the Court,
As mud between the beams thereof is wrought;
   And One who wrote on phosphates for the crops
Is subject-matter of his own Report.

[These be the glorious ends whereto we pass —
Let Him who Is, go call on Him who Was;
   And He shall see the *mallie* steals the slab
For currie-grinder, and for goats the grass.

A breath of wind, a Border bullet's flight,
A draught of water, or a horse's fright —
   The droning of the fat *Sheristadar*
Ceases, the punkah stops, and falls the night

For You or Me.   Do those who live decline
The step that offers, or their work resign?
   Trust me, To-day's Most Indispensables,
Five hundred men can take your place or mine.

OTHER VERSES

MY RIVAL

I GO to concert, party, ball —
  What profit is in these?
I sit alone against the wall
  And strive to look at ease.
The incense that is mine by right
  They burn before Her shrine;
And that's because I'm seventeen
  And she is forty-nine.

I cannot check my girlish blush,
  My colour comes and goes;
I redden to my finger-tips,
  And sometimes to my nose.
But She is white where white should be
  And red where red should shine.
The blush that flies at seventeen
  Is fixed at forty-nine.

I wish *I* had Her constant cheek:
  I wish that I could sing

53

All sorts of funny little songs,
   Not quite the proper thing.
I'm very *gauche* and very shy,
   Her jokes aren't in my line;
And, worst of all, I'm seventeen,
   While She is forty-nine.

The young men come, the young men go,
   Each pink and white and neat,
She's older than their mothers, but
   They grovel at Her feet.
They walk beside Her *'rickshaw*-wheels —
   They never walk by mine;
And that's because I'm seventeen
   And She is forty-nine.

She rides with half a dozen men
   (She calls them "boys" and "mashers"),
I trot along the Mall alone;
   My prettiest frocks and sashes
Don't help to fill my programme-card,
   And vainly I repine
From ten to two A. M.   Ah me!
   Would I were forty-nine.

She calls me "darling," "pet," and "dear,"
  And "sweet retiring maid."
I'm always at the back, I know,
  She puts me in the shade.
She introduces me to men,
  "Cast" lovers, I opine,
For sixty takes to seventeen,
  Nineteen to forty-nine.

But even She must older grow
  And end Her dancing days,
She can't go on for ever so
  At concerts, balls, and plays.
One ray of priceless hope I see
  Before my footsteps shine:
Just think, that She'll be eighty-one
  When I am forty-nine!

TO THE UNKNOWN GODDESS

WILL you conquer my heart with your beauty; my
    soul going out from afar?
Shall I fall to your hand as a victim of crafty and
    cautious *shikar?*

Have I met you and passed you already, unknow-
    ing, unthinking, and blind?
Shall I meet you next season at Simla, oh sweetest
    and best of your kind?

Does the P. and O. bear you to meward, or, clad
    in short frocks in the West,
Are you growing the charms that shall capture and
    torture the heart in my breast?

Will you stay in the Plains till September — my
    passion as warm as the day?
Will you bring me to book on the Mountains, or
    where the thermantidotes play?

When the light of your eyes shall make pallid the
    mean lesser lights I pursue,
And the charm of your presence shall lure me
    from love of the gay "thirteen-two":

When the peg and the pigskin shall please not;
    when I buy me Calcutta-built clothes;
When I quit the Delight of Wild Asses; forswearing
    the swearing of oaths;

As a deer to the hand of the hunter when I turn
    'mid the gibes of my friends;
When the days of my freedom are numbered, and
    the life of the bachelor ends.

Ah Goddess! child, spinster, or widow — as of old
    on Mars Hill when they raised
To the God that they knew not an altar — so I, a
    young Pagan, have praised

The Goddess I know not nor worship; yet, if half
    that men tell me be true,
You will come in the future, and therefore the
    verses are written to you!

THE RUPAIYAT OF OMAR KAL'VIN

[Allowing for the difference 'twixt prose and rhymed exaggeration, this ought to reproduce the sense of what Sir A —— told the nation some time ago, when the Government struck from our incomes two per cent.]

Now the New Year, reviving last Year's Debt,
The thoughtful Fisher casteth wide his Net;
   So I with begging Dish and ready Tongue
Assail all Men for all that — I can get.

Imports indeed are gone with all their Dues —
Lo! Salt a Lever that I dare not use,
   Nor may I ask the Tillers in Bengal —
Surely my Kith and Kin will not refuse

Pay — and I promise by the Dust of Spring,
Retrenchment. If my promises can bring
   Comfort, Ye have them now a thousand-fold —
By Allah! I will promise *Anything!*

Indeed, indeed, Retrenchment oft before
I swore — but did I mean it when I swore?
   And then, and then, We wandered to the Hills,
And so the Little Less became Much More.

Whether a Boileaugunge or Babylon,
I know not how the wretched Thing is done,
   The Items of Receipt grow surely small;
The Items of Expense mount one by one.

I cannot help it.   What have I to do
With One and Five, or Four, or Three, or Two?
   Let Scribes spit Blood and Sulphur as they please,
Or Statesmen call me foolish — Heed not you.

Behold, I promise — Anything You will.
Behold, I greet you with an empty Till —
   Ah! Fellow-Sinners, of your Charity
Seek not the Reason of the Dearth, but fill.

For if I sinned and fell, where lies the Gain
Of Knowledge?   Would it ease you of your Pain
   To know the tangled Threads of Revenue
I ravel deeper in a hopeless Skein?

"Who hath not Prudence"— what was it I said,
Of Her who paints her Eyes and tires Her Head,
    And jibes and mocks the People in the Street,
And fawns upon them for Her thriftless Bread?

Accursed is She of Eve's daughters — She
Hath cast off Prudence, and Her End shall be
    Destruction. . . . Brethren, of your Bounty grant
Some portion of your daily Bread to *Me*.

PAGETT, M.P.

The toad beneath the harrow knows
Exactly where each tooth-point goes;
The Butterfly upon the road
Preaches contentment to that toad.

PAGETT, M.P., was a liar, and a fluent liar there-
with,—
He spoke of the heat of India as the "Asian Solar
Myth";
Came on a four months' visit, to "study the East,"
in November.
And I got him to sign an agreement vowing to stay
till September.

March came in with the *köil*. Pagett was cool and
gay,
Called me a "bloated Brahmin," talked of my
"princely pay."
March went out with the roses. "Where is your
heat?" said he.
"Coming," said I to Pagett. "Skittles!" said
Pagett, M.P.

April opened with punkahs, coolies, and prickly-
heat,—

Pagett was dear to mosquitoes, sandflies found him a
treat.

He grew speckled and lumpy — hammered, I grieve
to say,

Aryan brothers who fanned him, in an illiberal way.

May set in with a dust-storm,— Pagett went down
with the sun.

All the delights of the season tickled him one by
one.

Imprimis — ten days' "liver"— due to his drinking
beer;

Later, a dose of fever — slight, but he called it
severe.

Dysent'ry touched him in June, after the *Chota
Bursat* —

Lowered his portly person — made him yearn to
depart.

He didn't call me a "Brahmin," or "bloated," or
"overpaid,"

But seemed to think it a wonder that any one ever
stayed.

July was a trifle unhealthy,— Pagett was ill with fear,

Called it the "Cholera Morbus," hinted that life was
    dear.

He babbled of "eastern exile," and mentioned his
    home with tears;

But I hadn't seen *my* children for close upon seven
    years.

We reached a hundred and twenty once in the Court
    at noon,

[I've mentioned Pagett was portly] Pagett went off
    in a swoon.

That was an end to the business; Pagett, the per-
    jured, fled

With a practical, working knowledge of "Solar
    Myths" in his head.

And I laughed as I drove from the station, but the
    mirth died out on my lips

As I thought of the fools like Pagett who write of
    their "Eastern trips,"

And the sneers of the travelled idiots who duly mis-
    govern the land,

And I prayed to the Lord to deliver another one into
    my hand.

LA NUIT BLANCHE

A much-discerning Public hold
The Singer generally sings
Of personal and private things,
And prints and sells his past for gold.

Whatever I may here disclaim,
The very clever folk I sing to
Will most indubitably cling to
Their pet delusion, just the same.

I HAD seen, as dawn was breaking
  And I staggered to my rest,
Tara Devi softly shaking
  From the Cart Road to the crest.
I had seen the spurs of Jakko
  Heave and quiver, swell and sink;
Was it Earthquake or tobacco,
  Day of Doom or Night of Drink?

In the full, fresh, fragrant morning
  I observed a camel crawl.

64

Laws of gravitation scorning,
　On the ceiling and the wall;
Then I watched a fender walking,
　And I heard gray leeches sing,
And a red-hot monkey talking
　Did not seem the proper thing.

Then a Creature, skinned and crimson,
　Ran about the floor and cried,
And they said I had the "jims" on,
　And they dosed me with bromide,
And they locked me in my bed-room —
　Me and one wee Blood Red Mouse —
Though I said:—"To give my head room
　"You had best unroof the house."

But my words were all unheeded,
　Though I told the grave M.D.
That the treatment really needed
　Was a dip in open sea
That was lapping just below me,
　Smooth as silver, white as snow,
And it took three men to throw me
　When I found I could not go.

Half the night I watched the Heavens
  Fizz like '81 champagne —
Fly to sixes and to sevens,
  Wheel and thunder back again;
And when all was peace and order
  Save one planet nailed askew,
Much I wept because my warden
  Would not let me set it true.

After frenzied hours of waiting,
  When the Earth and Skies were dumb
Pealed an awful voice dictating
  An interminable sum,
Changing to a tangled story —
  "What she said you said I said —"
Till the Moon arose in glory,
  And I found her . . . in my head;

Then a Face came, blind and weeping
  And It couldn't wipe Its eyes,
And It muttered I was keeping
  Back the moonlight from the skies;
So I patted It for pity,
  But It whistled shrill with wrath,
And a huge, black Devil City
  Poured its peoples on my path.

So I fled with steps uncertain
  On a thousand-year long race,
But the bellying of the curtain
  Kept me always in one place;
While the tumult rose and maddened
  To the roar of Earth on fire,
Ere it ebbed and sank and saddened
  To a whisper tense as wire.

In intolerable stillness
  Rose one little, little star,
And it chuckled at my illness,
  And it mocked me from afar;
And its brethren came and eyed me,
  Called the Universe to aid,
Till I lay, with naught to hide me,
  'Neath the Scorn of all Things Made.

Dun and saffron, robed and splendid
  Broke the solemn, pitying Day,
And I knew my pains were ended,
  And I turned and tried to pray;
But my speech was shattered wholly,
  And I wept as children weep,
Till the dawn-wind, softly, slowly,
  Brought to burning eyelids sleep.

THE LOVERS' LITANY

Eyes of gray — the sodden quay,
Driving rain and falling tears,
As the steamer heads to sea
In a parting storm of cheers.
　　Sing, for Faith and Hope are high.
　　None so true as you and I —
　　Sing the Lovers' Litany:—
　　"Love like ours can never die!"

Eyes of black — the throbbing keel
Milky foam to left and right;
Little whispers near the wheel
In the brilliant tropic night.
　　Cross that rules the Southern Sky,
　　Stars that sweep, and wheel, and fly,
　　Hear the Lovers' Litany:—
　　"Love like ours can never die!"

Eyes of brown — the dusty plain
Split and parched with heat of June.

Flying hoof and tightened rein,
Hearts that beat the old, old tune.
   Side by side the horses fly,
   Frame we now the old reply
   Of the Lovers' Litany:—
   "Love like ours can never die!"

Eyes of blue — the Simla Hills
Silvered with the moonlight hoar;
Pleading of the waltz that thrills,
Dies and echoes round Benmore.
   "Mabel," "Officers," "Good-bye,"
   Glamour, wine, and witchery —
   On my soul's sincerity,
   "Love like ours can never die!"

Maidens, of your charity,
Pity my most luckless state.
Four times Cupid's debtor I —
Bankrupt in quadruplicate.
   Yet, despite this evil case,
   And a maiden showed me grace,
   Four-and-forty times would I
   Sing the Lovers' Litany:—
   "Love like ours can never die!"

A BALLAD OF BURIAL

"Saint Praxed's ever was the Church for peace."

If down here I chance to die,
   Solemnly I beg you take
All that is left of "I"
   To the Hills for old sake's sake.
Pack, and pack me thoroughly,
   In the ice that used to slake
Drinks I drank when I was dry —
   This observe for old sake's sake.

To the railway station hie,
   There a single ticket take
For Umballa — goods-train — I
   Shall not mind delay or shake.
I shall rest contentedly
   Spite of clamour coolies make;
Thus in frozen dignity
   Send me up for old sake's sake.

70

Next the sleepy van Babu wake,
  Book a Kalka van "for four."
Few, I think, will care to make
  Journeys with me any more
As they used to do of yore.
  I shall need a "special" break —
Thing I never took before —
  Get me one for old sake's sake.

After that — arrangements make,
  No hotel will take me in,
And a bullock's back would break
  'Neath the teak and leaden skin.
Tonga-ropes are frail and thin,
  Or, did I a back seat take,
In a tonga I might spin,
  Do your best for old sake's sake.

After that — your work is done.
  Recollect a Padre must
Mourn the dear departed one —
  Throw the ashes and the dust.
Don't go down at once.   I trust
  You will find excuse to "snake

Three days' casual on the bust,"—
  Get your fun for old sake's sake.

I could never stand the Plains,
  Think of blazing June and May,
Think of those September rains
  Yearly till the Judgment Day!
I should never rest in peace,
  I should sweat and lie awake.
Rail me then, on my decease,
  To the Hills for old sake's sake.

THE OVERLAND MAIL

[Foot-service to the Hills]

In the name of the Empress of India, make way,
  O Lords of the Jungle, wherever you roam,
The woods are awake at the end of the day —
  We exiles are waiting for letters from Home.
Let the robber retreat — and the tiger turn tail —
In the Name of the Empress, the Overland Mail!

With a jingle of bells as the dusk gathers in,
  He turns to the foot-path that heads up the hill —
The bags on his back and a cloth round his chin,
  And, tucked in his waistbelt, the Post Office
    bill;—
"Despatched on this date, as received by the rail,
"*Per* runner, two bags of the Overland Mail."

Is the torrent in spate? He must ford it or swim.
  Has the rain wrecked the road? He must climb
    by the cliff.

Does the tempest cry halt?   What are tempests to
    him?
  The service admits not a "but" or an "if."
While the breath's in his mouth, he must bear
    without fail,
In the Name of the Empress, the Overland Mail.

From aloe to rose-oak, from rose-oak to fir,
  From level to upland, from upland to crest,
From rice-field to rock-ridge, from rock-ridge to spur,
  Fly the soft-sandalled feet, strains the scrawny
    brown chest.
From rail to ravine — to the peak from the vale —
Up, up through the night goes the Overland Mail.

There's a speck on the hill-side, a dot on the road —
  A jingle of bells on the foot-path below —
There's a scuffle above in the monkey's abode —
  The world is awake and the clouds are aglow.
For the great Sun himself must attend to the hail: —
"In the Name of the Empress, the Overland Mail!"

DIVIDED DESTINIES

IT was an artless *Bandar*, and he danced upon a pine,
And much I wondered how he lived, and where the
beast might dine,
And many, many other things, till, o'er my morning
smoke,
I slept the sleep of idleness and dreamt that *Bandar*
spoke.

He said:—"Oh man of many clothes!   Sad crawler
on the Hills!
"Observe, I know not Ranken's shop, nor Ranken's
monthly bills!
"I take no heed to trousers or the coats that you call
dress;
"Nor am I plagued with little cards for little drinks
at Mess.

"I steal the bunnia's grain at morn, at noon and
eventide
"(For he is fat and I am spare), I roam the mountain
side,

"I follow no man's carriage, and no, never in my life
"Have I flirted at Peliti's with another *Bandar's* wife.

"Oh man of futile fopperies — unnecessary wraps;
"I own no ponies in the hills, I drive no tall-wheeled
traps.
"I buy me not twelve-button gloves, 'short-sixes'
eke, of rings,
"Nor do I waste at Hamilton's my wealth on pretty
things.

"I quarrel with my wife at home, we never fight
abroad;
"But Mrs. B. has grasped the fact I am her only lord.
"I never heard of fever — dumps nor debts depress
my soul;
"And I pity and despise you!" Here he pouched
my breakfast-roll.

His hide was very mangy and his face was very red,
And undisguisedly he scratched with energy his head.
His manners were not always nice, but how my spirit
cried
To be an artless *Bandar* loose upon the mountain
side!

So I answered:—"Gentle *Bandar*, an inscrutable
 Decree,

"Makes thee a gleesome fleasome Thou, and me a
 wretched Me.

"Go! Depart in peace, my brother, to thy home
 amid the pine;

"Yet forget not once a mortal wished to change his
 lot with thine."

THE MASQUE OF PLENTY

ARGUMENT.— The Indian Government being minded to
discover the economic condition of their lands, sent a Com-
mittee to inquire into it; and saw that it was good.

SCENE.— *The wooded heights of Simla. The Incarnation of the Government of India in the raiment
of the Angel of Plenty sings, to pianoforte ac-
companiment:—*

"How sweet is the shepherd's sweet life!
From the dawn to the even he strays —
He shall follow his sheep all the day
And his tongue shall be filled with praise.

(*adagio dim.*) Fillèd with praise!"

(*largendo con sp.*) Now this is the position,
Go make an inquisition
Into their real condition
As swiftly as ye may.

(*p*) Ay, paint our swarthly billions
The richest of vermilions
Ere two well-led cotillions
Have danced themselves away.

78

TURKISH PATROL, *as able and intelligent Investigators
wind down the Himalayas:—*

What is the state of the Nation?   What is its occupa-
tion?

Hi! get along, get along, get along, — lend us the
information!

(*dim.*) Census the *bylu* and the *yaba* — capture a
first-class Babu,

Set him to cut Gazetteers — Gazetteers . . .

(*ff*) What is the state of the Nation, &c., &c.

INTERLUDE, *from Nowhere in Particular, to stringed
and Oriental instruments.*

Our cattle reel beneath the yoke they bear —
  The earth is iron and the skies are brass —
And faint with fervour of the flaming air
  The languid hours pass.

Our wells are dry beneath the village tree —
  The young wheat withers ere it reach a span,
And belts of blinding sand show cruelly
  Where once the river ran.

Pray, brothers, pray, but to no earthly King —
  Lift up your hands above the blighted grain,

Look westward — if They please, the Gods shall bring
  Their mercy with the Rain.

Look westward — bears the blue no brown cloud-
    bank?
  Nay, it is written — wherefore should we fly?
On our own field and by our cattle's flank
  Lie down, lie down to die!

SEMI-CHORUS.

By the plumed heads of Kings
            Waving high,
Where the tall corn springs
            O'er the dead.
If they rust or rot we die,
If they ripen we are fed.
Very mighty is the power of our Kings!

*Triumphal return to Simla of the Investigators, at-
tired after the manner of Dionysus, leading a pet
tiger-cub in wreaths of rhubarb leaves, symbolical of
India under medical treatment.   They sing:—*

We have seen, we have written — behold it, the
    proof of our manifold toil!
In their hosts they assembled and told it — the tale
    of the Sons of the Soil.

We have said of the Sickness —"Where is it?"—
    and of Death —"It is far from our ken,"—
We have paid a particular visit to the affluent chil-
    dren of men.
We have trodden the mart and the well-curb — we
    have stooped to the bield and the byre;
And the King may the forces of Hell curb — for the
    People have all they desire!

Castanets and step-dance:

Oh, the *dom* and the *mag* and the *thakur* and the *thag,*
    And the *nat* and the *brinjaree,*
And the *bunnia* and the *ryot* are as happy and as quiet
    And as plump as they can be!
Yes, the *jain* and the *jat* in his stucco-fronted hut,
    And the bounding *bazugar,*
By the favour of the King, are as fat as anything,
    They are — they are — they are!

RECITATIVE, *Government of India, with white satin
    wings and electroplated harp:*—

How beautiful upon the mountains — in peace reclin-
    ing,
Thus to be assured that our people are unanimously
    dining.
And though there are places not so blessed as others

in natural advantages, which, after all, was only
    to be expected,
Proud and glad are we to congratulate you upon the
    work you have thus ably effected.

CHORUS OF THE CRYSTALLIZED FACTS.
Before the beginning of years
There came to the rule of the State
Men with a pair of shears,
Men with an Estimate —
Strachey with Muir for leaven,
Lytton with locks that fell,
Ripon fooling with Heaven,
And Temple riding like H—ll!
And the bigots took in hand
Cess and the falling of rain,
And the measure of sifted sand
The dealer puts in the grain —
Imports by land and sea,
To uttermost decimal worth,
And registration — free —
In the Houses of Death and of Birth:
And fashioned with pens and paper,
And fashioned in black and white,
With Life for a flickering taper

And Death for a blazing light —
With the Armed and the Civil Power,
That his strength might endure for a span
From Adam's Bridge to Peshawur,
The Much Administered Man.

In the towns of the North and the East,
They gathered as unto rule,
They bade him starve his priest
And send his children to school.
Railways and roads they wrought,
For the needs of the trade within;
A time to squabble in court,
A time to bear and to grin;
And gave him peace in his ways,
Jails — and Police to fight,
Justice at length of days,
And Right — and Might in the Right.
His speech is of mortgaged bedding,
On his kine he borrows yet,
At his heart is his daughter's wedding,
In his eye foreknowledge of debt.
He eats and hath indigestion,
He toils and he may not stop;
His life is a long-drawn question
Between a crop and a crop.

THE MARE'S NEST

JANE Austen Beecher Stowe de Rouse
　　Was good beyond all earthly need;
But, on the other hand, her spouse
　　Was very, very bad indeed.
He smoked cigars, called churches slow,
And raced — but this she did not know.

For Belial Machiavelli kept
　　The little fact a secret, and,
Though o'er his minor sins she wept,
　　Jane Austen did not understand
That Lilly — thirteen-two and bay —
Absorbed one half her husband's pay.

She was so good she made him worse
　　(Some women are like this, I think);
He taught her parrot how to curse,
　　Her Assam monkey how to drink.
He vexed her righteous soul until
She went up, and he went down hill.

Then came the crisis, strange to say,
   Which turned a good wife to a better.
A telegraphic peon, one day,
   Brought her — now, had it been a letter
For Belial Machiavelli, I
Know Jane would just have let it lie.

But 'twas a telegram instead,
   Marked "urgent," and her duty plain
To open it.   Jane Austen read:—
   "Your Lilly's got a cough again.
"Can't understand why she is kept
"At your expense."   Jane Austen wept.

It was a misdirected wire,
   Her husband was at Shaitanpore.
She spread her anger, hot as fire,
   Through six thin foreign sheets or more,
Sent off that letter, wrote another
To her solicitor — and mother.

Then Belial Machiavelli saw
   Her error and, I trust, his own,
Wired to the minion of the Law,
   And travelled wifeward — not alone:

For Lilly — thirteen-two and bay —
Came in a horse-box all the way.

There was a scene — a weep or two —
   With many kisses.   Austen Jane
Rode Lilly all the season through,
   And never opened wires again.
She races now with Belial.   This
Is very sad, but so it is.

THE BALLAD OF FISHER'S BOARDING
HOUSE

That night when through the mooring chains
  The wide-eyed corpse rolled free,
To blunder down by Garden Reach
  And rot at Kedgeree,
The tale the Hughli told the shoal
  The lean shoal whispered me.

'TWAS Fultah Fisher's boarding-house,
  Where sailor-men reside,
And there were men of all the ports
  From Mississip to Clyde,
And regally they spat and smoked,
  And fearsomely they lied.

They lied about the purple Sea
  That gave them scanty bread,
They lied about the Earth beneath,
  The Heavens overhead,
For they had looked too often on
  Black rum when that was red.

And there was Hans the Blue-eyed Dane,
    Bull-throated, bare of arm,
Who carried on his hairy chest
    The maid Ultruda's charm —
The little silver crucifix
    That keeps a man from harm.

And there was Jake Without-the-Ears,
    And Pamba the Malay,
And Carboy Gin the Guinea cook,
    And Luz from Vigo Bay,
And Honest Jack who sold them slops
    And harvested their pay.

And there was Salem Hardieker,
    A lean Bostonian he —
Russ, German, English, Halfbreed, Finn,
    Yank, Dane and Portugee,
At Fultah's Fisher's boarding-place
    They rested from the sea

Now Anne of Austria shared their drinks,
    Collinga knew her fame,
From Tarnau in Galicia
    To Jaun Bazar she came,

To eat the bread of infamy
  And take the wage of shame.

She held a dozen men to heel —
  Rich spoil of war was hers,
In hose and gown and ring and chain,
  From twenty mariners,
And, by Port Law, that week, men called
  Her Salem Hardieker's.

But seamen learnt — what landsmen know —
  That neither gifts nor gain
Can hold a winking Light o' Love
  Or Fancy's flight restrain,
When Anne of Austria rolled her eyes
  On Hans the blue-eyed Dane.

Since Life is strife, and strife means knife,
  From Howrah to the Bay,
And he may die before the dawn
  Who liquored out the day,
In Fultah Fisher's boarding-house
  We woo while yet we may.

But cold was Hans the blue-eyed Dane,
  Bull-throated, bare of arm,

And laughter shook the chest beneath
  The maid Ultruda's charm —
The little silver crucifix
  That keeps a man from harm.

"You speak to Salem Hardieker,
  "You was his girl, I know.
"I ship mineselfs to-morrow, see,
  "Und round the Skaw we go,
"South, down the Cattegat, by Hjelm,
  "To Besser in Saro."

When love rejected turns to hate,
  All ill betide the man.
"You speak to Salem Hardieker"—
  She spoke as woman can.
A scream—a sob—"He called me — names!"
  And then the fray began.

An oath from Salem Hardieker,
  A shriek upon the stairs,
A dance of shadows on the wall,
  A knife-thrust unawares —
And Hans came down, as cattle drop,
  Across the broken chairs.

        .   .   .   .

In Anne of Austria's trembling hands
　　The weary head fell low:—
"I ship mineselfs to-morrow, straight
　　"For Besser in Saro;
"Und there Ultruda comes to me
　　"At Easter, und I go.

"South, down the Cattegat —What's here?
　　"There — are — no — lights —to — guide!"
The mutter ceased, the spirit passed,
　　And Anne of Austria cried
In Fultah Fisher's boarding-house
　　When Hans the mighty died.

Thus slew they Hans the blue-eyed Dane,
　　Bull-throated, bare of arm,
But Anne of Austria looted first
　　The maid Ultruda's charm —
The little silver crucifix
　　That keeps a man from harm.

POSSIBILITIES

Ay, lay him 'neath the Simla pine —
   A fortnight fully to be missed,
   Behold, we lose our fourth at whist,
A chair is vacant where we dine.

His place forgets him; other men
   Have bought his ponies, guns, and traps.
   His fortune is the Great Perhaps
And that cool rest-house down the glen,

Whence he shall hear, as spirits may,
   Our mundane revel on the height,
   Shall watch each flashing *'rickshaw*-light
Sweep on to dinner, dance, and play.

Benmore shall woo him to the ball
   With lighted rooms and braying band:
   And he shall hear and understand
"Dream Faces" better than us all.

For, think you, as the vapours flee
   Across Sanjaolie after rain,

His soul may climb the hill again
To each old field of victory.

Unseen, who women held so dear,
    The strong man's yearning to his kind
    Shall shake at most the window-blind,
Or dull awhile the card-room's cheer.

In his own place of power unknown,
    His Light o' Love another's flame,
    His dearest pony galloped lame,
And he an alien and alone.

Yet may he meet with many a friend —
    Shrewd shadows, lingering long unseen
    Among us when "*God save the Queen*"
Shows even "extras" have an end.

And, when we leave the heated room,
    And, when at four the lights expire,
    The crew shall gather round the fire
And mock our laughter in the gloom.

Talk as we talked, and they ere death —
    First wanly, danced in ghostly wise,
    With ghosts of tunes for melodies,
And vanished at the morning's breath!

ARITHMETIC ON THE FRONTIER

A GREAT and glorious thing it is
   To learn, for seven years or so,
The Lord knows what of that and this,
   Ere reckoned fit to face the foe —
The flying bullet down the Pass,
That whistles clear:—"All flesh is grass."

Three hundred pounds per annum spent
   On making brain and body meeter
For all the murderous intent
   Comprised in "villanous saltpeter!"
And after?— Ask the Yusufzaies
What comes of all our 'ologies.

A scrimmage in a Border Station —
   A canter down some dark defile —
Two thousand pounds of education
   Drops to a ten-rupee *jezail* —
The Crammer's boast, the Squadron's pride,
Shot like a rabbit in a ride!

No proposition Euclid wrote,
  No formulæ the text-books know,
Will turn the bullet from your coat,
  Or ward the tulwar's downward blow.
Strike hard who cares—shoot straight who can—
The odds are on the cheaper man.

One sword-knot stolen from the camp
  Will pay for all the school-expenses
Of any Kurrum Valley scamp
  Who knows no word of moods and tenses,
But, being blest with perfect sight,
Picks off our messmates left and right.

With home-bred hordes the hill-sides teem,
  The troop-ships bring us one by one,
At vast expense of time and steam,
  To slay Afridis where they run.
The "captives of our bow and spear"
Are cheap, alas! as we are dear.

THE SONG OF THE WOMEN

*(Lady Dufferin's Fund for Medical Aid to the Women
of India.)*

How shall she know the worship we would do her?
   The walls are high and she is very far.
How shall the women's message reach unto her
    Above the tumult of the packed bazar?
      Free wind of March, against the lattice blowing,
      Bear thou our thanks lest she depart unknowing.

Go forth across the fields we may not roam in,
   Go forth beyond the trees that rim the city
To whatsoe'er fair place she hath her home in,
    Who dowered us with wealth of love and pity.
      Out of our shadow pass and seek her singing —
      "I have no gifts but Love alone for bringing."

Say that we be a feeble folk who greet her,
   But old in grief, and very wise in tears;
Say that we, being desolate, entreat her
    That she forget us not in after years;

For we have seen the light, and it were grievous
To dim that dawning if our lady leave us.

By life that ebbed with none to staunch the failing,
  By Love's sad harvest garnered in the spring,
When Love in Ignorance wept unavailing
  O'er young buds dead before their blossoming;
    By all the gray owl watched—the pale moon
      viewed,
    In past grim years declare our gratitude!

By hands uplifted to the Gods that heard not,
  By gifts that found no favour in Their sight,
By faces bent above the babe that stirred not,
  By nameless horrors of the stifling night;
    By ills foredone, by peace her toils discover,
    Bid Earth be good beneath and Heaven above
      her!

If she have sent her servants in our pain,
  If she have fought with Death and dulled his sword;
If she have given back our sick again,
  And to the breast the weakling lips restored,
    Is it a little thing that she has wrought?
    Then Life and Death and Motherhood be naught.

Go forth, O wind, our message on thy wings,
  And they shall hear thee pass and bid thee speed,
In reed-roofed hut, or white-walled home of kings,
  Who have been holpen by her in their need.
    All spring shall give thee fragrance, and the wheat
    Shall be a tasselled floorcloth to thy feet.

Haste, for our hearts are with thee, take no rest!
  Loud-voiced ambassador, from sea to sea
Proclaim the blessing, manifold, confest,
  Of those in darkness by her hand set free,
    Then very softly to her presence move,
    And whisper: "Lady, lo, they know and love!"

THE BETROTHED

"You must choose between me and your cigar."

Open the old cigar-box, get me a Cuba stout,
For things are running crossways, and Maggie and I
    are out.

We quarrelled about Havanas — we fought o'er a
    good cheroot,
And I know she is exacting, and she says I am a
    brute.

Open the old cigar-box — let me consider a space;
In the soft blue veil of the vapour musing on Maggie's
    face.

Maggie is pretty to look at — Maggie's a loving lass,
But the prettiest cheeks must wrinkle, the truest of
    loves must pass.

There's peace in a Laranaga, there's calm in a Henry
    Clay,
But the best cigar in an hour is finished and thrown
    away —

Thrown away for another as perfect and ripe and
    brown —
But I could not throw away Maggie for fear o' the
    talk o' the town!

Maggie, my wife at fifty — gray and dour and old —
With never another Maggie to purchase for love or
    gold!

And the light of Days that have Been the dark of
    the Days that Are,
And Love's torch stinking and stale, like the butt of
    a dead cigar —

The butt of a dead cigar you are bound to keep in
    your pocket —
With never a new one to light tho' it's charred and
    black to the socket.

Open the old cigar-box — let me consider awhile —
Here is a mild Manilla — there is a wifely smile.

Which is the better portion — bondage bought with
    a ring,
Or a harem of dusky beauties fifty tied in a string?

Counsellors cunning and silent — comforters true
    and tried,
And never a one of the fifty to sneer at a rival bride.

Thought in the early morning, solace in time of woes,
Peace in the hush of the twilight, balm ere my
    eyelids close.

This will the fifty give me, asking naught in return,
With only a *Suttee's* passion — to do their duty and
    burn.

This will the fifty give me. When they are spent
    and dead,
Five times other fifties shall be my servants instead.

The furrows of far-off Java, the isles of the Spanish
    Main,
When they hear my harem is empty, will send me
    my brides again.

I will take no heed to their raiment, nor food for
    their mouths withal,
So long as the gulls are nesting, so long as the showers
    fall.

I will scent 'em with best Vanilla, with tea will I
    temper their hides,
And the Moor and the Mormon shall envy who read
    of the tale of my brides.

For Maggie has written a letter that gives me my
    choice between
The wee little whimpering Love and the great god
    Nick o' Teen.

And I have been servant of Love for barely a twelve-
    month clear,
But I have been Priest of Partagas a matter of
    seven year;

And the gloom of my bachelor days is flecked with
    the cheery light
Of stumps that I burned to Friendship and Pleasure
    and Work and Fight.

And I turn my eyes to the future that Maggie and
    I must prove,
But the only light on the marshes is the Will-o'-the-
    Wisp of Love.

Will it see me safe through my journey or leave me
    bogged in the mire?
Since a puff of tobacco can cloud it, shall I follow the
    fitful fire?

Open the old cigar-box — let me consider anew —
Old friends, and who is Maggie that I should aban-
    don *you?*

A million surplus Maggies are willing to bear the yoke;
And a woman is only a woman, but a good cigar is
    a Smoke.

Light me another Cuba — I hold to my first-sworn
    vows,
If Maggie will have no rival, I'll have no Maggie for
    spouse!

A BALLADE OF JAKKO HILL

ONE moment bid the horses wait,
   Since tiffin is not laid till three,
Below the upward path and strait
   You climbed a year ago with me.
Love came upon us suddenly
   And loosed — an idle hour to kill —
A headless, harmless armoury
   That smote us both on Jakko Hill.

Ah Heaven! we would wait and wait
   Through Time and to Eternity!
Ah Heaven! we would conquer Fate
   With more than Godlike constancy!
I cut the date upon a tree —
   Here stand the clumsy figures still:—
" 10-7-85, A.D."
   Damp with the mist on Jakko Hill.

What came of high resolve and great,
   And until Death fidelity?

Whose horse is waiting at your gate?
   Whose 'rickshaw-wheels ride over me?
No Saint's, I swear; and — let me see
   To-night what names your programme fill —
We drift asunder merrily,
   As drifts the mist on Jakko Hill!

L'envoi

Woman, behold our ancient state
   Has clean departed; and we see
'Twas Idleness we took for Fate
   That bound light bonds on you and me.
Amen!   Here ends the comedy
   Where it began in all good will,
Since Love and Leave together flee
   As driven mist on Jakko Hill!

THE PLEA OF THE SIMLA DANCERS

Too late, alas! the song
To remedy the wrong;—
The rooms are taken from us, swept and garnished for
their fate
But these tear-besprinkled pages
Shall attest to future ages
That we cried against the crime of it — too late, alas!
too late!

"WHAT have *we* ever done to bear this grudge?"
  Was there no room save only in Benmore
For docket, *duftar*, and for office drudge,
  That you usurp our smoothest dancing floor?
Must babus do their work on polished teak?
  Are ball-rooms fittest for the ink you spill?
Was there no other cheaper house to seek?
  You might have left them all at Strawberry Hill

We never harmed you! Innocent our guise,
  Dainty our shining feet, our voices low;

106

And we revolved to divers melodies,
  And we were happy but a year ago.
To-night the moon that watched our lightsome wiles —
  That beamed upon us through the deodars —
Is wan with gazing on official files,
  And desecrating desks disgust the stars.

Nay! by the memory of tuneful nights —
  Nay! by the witchery of flying feet —
Nay! by the glamour of foredone delights —
  By all things merry, musical, and meet —
By wine that sparkled, and by sparkling eyes —
  By wailing waltz — by reckless gallop's strain —
By dim verandahs and by soft replies,
  Give us our ravished ball-room back again!

Or — hearken to the curse we lay on you!
  The ghosts of waltzes shall perplex your brain,
And murmurs of past merriment pursue
  Your 'wildered clerks that they indite in vain;
And when you count your poor Provincial millions,
  The only figures that your pen shall frame
Shall be the figures of dear, dear cotillons
  Danced out in tumult long before you came.

Yea! "*See Saw*" shall upset your estimates,
  "*Dream-faces*" shall your heavy heads bemuse.
Because your hand, unheeding, desecrates
  Our temple; fit for higher, worthier use.
And all the long verandahs, eloquent
  With echoes of a score of Simla years,
Shall plague you with unbidden sentiment —
  Babbling of kisses, laughter, love, and tears.

So shall you mazed amid old memories stand,
  So shall you toil, and shall accomplish naught.
And ever in your ears a phantom Band
  Shall blare away the staid official thought.
Wherefore — and ere this awful curse be spoken,
  Cast out your swarthy, sacrilegious train,
And give — ere dancing cease and hearts be broken —
  Give us our ravished ball-room back again!

"AS THE BELL CLINKS"

As I left the Halls at Lumley, rose the vision of a
    comely
Maid last season worshipped dumbly, watched with
    fervour from afar;
And I wondered idly, blindly, if the maid would greet
    me kindly.
That was all — the rest was settled by the clinking
    tonga-bar.
Ay, my life and hers were coupled by the tonga
    coupling bar.

For my misty meditation, at the second changing-
    station,
Suffered sudden dislocation, fled before the tuneless
    jar
Of a Wagner *obbligato*, *scherzo*, double-hand *staccato*,
Played on either pony's saddle by the clacking
    tonga-bar —
Played with human speech, I fancied, by the jigging,
    jolting bar.

"She was sweet," thought I, "last season, but 'twere
  surely wild unreason
"Such a tiny hope to freeze on as was offered by my
  Star,
"When she whispered, something sadly:—'I — we
  feel your going badly?'"
"*And you let the chance escape you?*" rapped the
  rattling tonga-bar.
"*What a chance and what an idiot!*" clicked the
  vicious tonga-bar.

Heart of man — Oh heart of putty! Had I gone
  by Kakahutti,
On the old Hill-road and rutty, I had 'scaped that
  fatal car:
But his fortune each must bide by, so I watched the
  milestones slide by.
To —"*You call on Her to-morrow!*"— fugue with
  cymbals by the bar —
"*You must call on Her to-morrow!*"— post-horn
  gallop by the bar.

Yet a further stage my goal on — we were whirling
  down to Solon,
With a double lurch and roll on, best foot foremost,
  ganz und gar —

"She was *very* sweet," I hinted.   "If a kiss had been
    imprinted ——?"

"*Would ha' saved a world of trouble!*" clashed the
    busy tonga-bar.

"*'Been accepted or rejected!*" banged and clanged
    the tonga-bar.

Then a notion wild and daring, 'spite the income
    tax's paring

And a hasty thought of sharing — less than many
    incomes are

Made me put a question private, you can guess what
    I would drive at.

"*You must work the sum to prove it,*" clanked the
    careless tonga-bar.

"*Simple Rule of Two will prove it,*" lilted back the
    tonga-bar.

It was under Khyraghaut I mused:— Suppose the
    maid be haughty —

"[There are lovers rich — and forty] wait some
    wealthy Avatar?

"Answer, monitor untiring, 'twixt the ponies twain
    perspiring!"

"*Faint heart never won fair lady,*" creaked the
    straining tonga-bar.
"*Can I tell you ere you ask Her?*" pounded slow the
    tonga-bar.

Last, the Tara Devi turning showed the lights of
    Simla burning,
Lit my little lazy yearning to a fiercer flame by far.
As below the Mall we jingled, through my very heart
    it tingled —
The reiterated order of the threshing tonga-bar:—
"*Try your luck — you can't do better!*" twanged the
    loosened tonga-bar.

CHRISTMAS IN INDIA

Dim dawn behind the tamarisks—the sky is saffron-
 yellow—
As the women in the village grind the corn,
And the parrots seek the river-side, each calling to
 his fellow
That the Day, the staring Eastern Day, is born.
 Oh the white dust on the highway! Oh the
 stenches in the byway!
 Oh the clammy fog that hovers over earth!
 And at Home they're making merry 'neath the
 white and scarlet berry—
 What part have India's exiles in their mirth?

Full day behind the tamarisks — the sky is blue and
 staring—
As the cattle crawl afield beneath the yoke,
And they bear One o'er the field-path who is past all
 hope or caring,
To the ghât below the curling wreaths of smoke.

Call on Rama, going slowly, as ye bear a brother
   lowly —
   Call on Rama — he may hear, perhaps, your
      voice!
With our hymnbooks and our psalters we appeal
   to other altars,
   And to-day we bid "good Christian men
      rejoice!"

High noon behind the tamarisks — the sun is hot
   above us —
As at Home the Christmas Day is breaking wan.
They will drink our healths at dinner — those who
   tell us how they love us,
   And forget us till another year be gone!
   Oh the toil that knows no breaking! Oh the
      heimweh, ceaseless, aching!
      Oh the black dividing Sea and alien Plain!
   Youth was cheap — wherefore we sold it.
   Gold was good — we hoped to hold it,
   And to-day we know the fulness of our gain.

Gray dusk behind the tamarisks — the parrots fly
   together —
As the Sun is sinking slowly over Home,

And his last ray turns to jeer us shackled in a life-
    long tether
That drags us back howe'er so far we roam.
    Hard her service, poor her payment — she in
        ancient, tattered raiment —
      India, she the grim stepmother of our kind.
    If a year of life be lent her, if her temple's
        shrine we enter,
      The door is shut — we may not look behind.

Black night behind the tamarisks — the owls begin
    their chorus —
    As the conches from the temple scream and bray.
With the fruitless years behind us and the hopeless
    years before us,
    Let us honour, oh my brothers, Christmas Day!
    Call a truce, then, to our labours — let us feast
        with friends and neighbours,
      And be merry as the custom of our caste;
    For, if "faint and forced the laughter," and if
        sadness follow after,
      We are richer by one mocking Christmas past.

THE GRAVE OF THE HUNDRED HEAD

THERE'S *a widow in sleepy Chester*
  Who weeps for her only son;
There's a grave on the Pabeng River,
  A grave that the Burmans shun,
And there's Subadar Prag Tewarri
  Who tells how the work was done.

A Snider squibbed in the jungle —
  Somebody laughed and fled,
And the men of the First Shikaris
  Picked up their Subaltern dead,
With a big blue mark in his forehead
And the back blown out of his head.

Subadar Prag Tewarrl,
  Jemadar Hira Lal,
Took command of the party,
  Twenty rifles in all;
Marched them down to the river
  As the day was beginning to fall.

They buried the boy by the river,
  A blanket over his face —
They wept for their dead Lieutenant,
  The men of an alien race —
They made a *samâdh* in his honour,
  A mark for his resting place.

For they swore by the Holy Water,
  They swore by the salt they ate,
That the soul of Lieutenant Eshmitt Sahib
  Should go to his God in state;
With fifty file of Burman
  To open him Heaven's gate.

The men of the First Shikaris
  Marched till the break of day,
Till they came to the rebel village,
  The village of Pabengmay —
A *jingal* covered the clearing,
  Calthrops hampered the way.

Subadar Prag Tewarri,
  Bidding them load with ball,
Halted a dozen rifles
  Under the village-wall;

Sent out a flanking party
  With Jemadar Hira Lal.

The men of the First Shikaris
  Shouted and smote and slew,
Turning the grinning *jingal*
  On to the howling crew.
The Jemadar's flanking-party
  Butchered the folk who flew.

Long was the morn of slaughter,
  Long was the list of slain,
Five score heads were taken
  Five score heads and twain;
And the men of the First Shikaris
  Went back to their grave again;

Each man bearing a basket
  Red as his palms that day,
Red as the blazing village —
  The village of Pabengmay.
And the "*drip-drip-drip*" from the baskets
  Reddened the grass by the way.

They made a pile of their trophies
  High as a tall man's chin,

Head upon head distorted,
   Clinched in a sightless grin,
Anger and pain and terror
   Writ on the smoke-scorched skin.

Subadar Prag Tewarri
   Set the head of the Boh
On the top of the mound of triumph
   The head of his son below,
With the sword and the peacock-banner
   That the world might behold and know.

Thus the *samádh* was perfect,
   Thus was the lesson plain
Of the wrath of the First Shikaris —
   The price of a white man slain;
And the men of the First Shikaris
   Went back into camp again.

Then a silence came to the river,
   A hush fell over the shore,
And Bohs that were brave departed,
   And Sniders squibbed no more;
     For the Burmans said
     That a *kullah's* head
Must be paid for with heads five score.

There's a widow in sleepy Chester
    Who weeps for her only son;
There's a grave on the Pabeng River,
    A grave that the Burmans shun,
And there's Subadar Prag Tewarri
    Who tells how the work was done.

AN OLD SONG

So long as 'neath the Kalka hills
   The tonga-horn shall ring,
So long as down the Solon dip
   The hard-held ponies swing;
So long as Tara Devi sees
   The lights o' Simla town,
So long as Pleasure calls us up,
   And duty drives us down,
     If you love me as I love you
     What pair so happy as we two?

So long as Aces take the King,
   Or backers take the bet,
So long as debt leads men to wed;
   Or marriage leads to debt;
So long as little luncheons, Love,
   And scandal hold their vogue,
While there is sport at Annandale
   Or whiskey at Jutogh,
     If you love me as I love you
     What knife can cut our love in two?

So long as down the rocking floor
  The raving polka spins,
So long as Kitchen Lancers spur
  The maddened violins;
So long as through the whirling smoke
  We hear the oft-told tale:—
"Twelve hundred in the Lotteries,"
  And *Whatshername* for sale?
    If you love me as I love you
    We'll play the game and win it too.

So long as Lust or Lucre tempt
  Straight riders from the course,
So long as with each drink we pour
  Black brewage of Remorse;
So long as those unloaded guns
  We keep beside the bed,
Blow off, by obvious accident,
  The lucky owner's head,
    If you love me as I love you
    What can Life kill or Death undo?

So long as Death 'twixt dance and dance
  Chills best and bravest blood

And drops the reckless rider down
   The rotten, rain-soaked *khud;*
So long as rumours from the North
   Make loving wives afraid,
So long as Burma claims the boy,
   And typhoid kills the maid,
     If you love me as I love you
     What knife can cut our love in two?

By all that lights our daily life
   Or works our lifelong woe,
From Boileaugunge to Simla Downs
   And those grim glades below,
Where heedless of the flying hoof
   And clamour overhead,
Sleep, with the gray-langur for guard
   Our very scornful Dead,
     If you love me as I love you
     All Earth is servant to us two!

By Docket, Billetdoux, and File,
   By Mountain, Cliff, and Fir,
By Fan and Sword and Office-box,
   By Corset, Plume, and Spur;

By Riot, Revel, Waltz, and War,
  By Woman, Work, and Bills,
By all the life that fizzes in
  The everlasting Hills,
    If you love me as I love you
    What pair so happy as we two?

CERTAIN MAXIMS OF HAFIZ

1

If It be pleasant to look on, stalled in the packed
   serai,

Does not the Young Man try Its temper and pace
   ere he buy?

If She be pleasant to look on, what does the Young
   Man say?

"Lo! She is pleasant to look on, give Her to me
   to-day!"

2

Yea, though a Kafir die, to him is remitted Jehannum

If he borrowed in life from a native at sixty per cent.
   per annum.

3

Blister we not for *bursati?* So when the heart is vext,

The pain of one maiden's refusal is drowned in the
   pain of the next.

4

The temper of chums, the love of your wife, and a
new piano's tune—
Which of the three will you trust at the end of an
Indian June?

5

Who are the rulers of Ind — to whom shall we bow
the knee?
Make your peace with the women, and men will
make you L. G.

6

Does the woodpecker flit round the young *ferash?*
Does grass clothe a new-built wall?
Is she under thirty the woman who holds a boy in
her thrall?

7

If She grows suddenly gracious — reflect.   Is it all
for thee?
The blackbuck is stalked through the bullock, and
Man through jealousy.

8

Seek not for favour of women.   So shall you find it
indeed.
Does not the boar break cover just when you're
lighting a weed?

9

If He play, being young and unskilful, for shekels of
    silver and gold,
Take His money, my son, praising Allah.   The kid
    was ordained to be sold.

10

With a "weed" among men or horses verily this is
    the best,
That you work him in office or dog-cart lightly — but
    give him no rest.

11

Pleasant the snaffle of Courtship, improving the
    manners and carriage,
But the colt who is wise will abstain from the terrible
    thorn-bit of Marriage;

12

As the thriftless gold of the *babul* so is the gold that
    we spend
On a Derby Sweep, or our neighbour's wife or the
    horse that we buy from a friend.

13

The ways of man with a maid be strange, yet simple
    and tame

To the ways of a man with a horse, when selling or
    racing that same.

14

In public Her face turneth to thee, and pleasant
    Her smile when ye meet.

It is ill.   The cold rocks of El-Gidar smile thus on
    the waves at their feet.

In public Her face is averted, with anger She nameth
    thy name.

It is well.   Was there ever a loser content with the
    loss of the game?

15

If She have spoken a word, remember thy lips are
    sealed,

And the Brand of the Dog is upon him by whom is
    the secret revealed.

If She have written a letter, delay not an instant but
    burn it.

Tear it in pieces, O Fool, and the wind to her mate
    shall return it!

If there be trouble to Herward, and a lie of the
blackest can clear,
Lie, while thy lips can move or a man is alive to hear.

16

My Son, if a maiden deny thee and scufflingly bid
thee give o'er,
Yet lip meets with lip at the lastward — get out!
She has been there before.
They are pecked on the ear and the chin and the
nose who are lacking in lore.

17

If we fall in the race, though we win, the hoof-slide
is scarred on the course
Though Allah and Earth pardon Sin, remaineth for
ever Remorse.

18

"By all I am misunderstood!" if the Matron shall
say, or the Maid:—
"Alas! I do not understand," my son, be thou nowise
afraid.
In vain in the sight of the Bird is the net of the
Fowler displayed.

19

My son, if I, Hafiz, thy father, take hold of thy
  knees in my pain,
Demanding thy name on stamped paper, one day
  or one hour — refrain.
Are the links of thy fetters so light that thou cravest
  another man's chain?

THE MOON OF OTHER DAYS

BENEATH the deep verandah's shade,
  When bats begin to fly,
I sit me down and watch — alas
  Another evening die.
Blood-red behind the sere *ferash*
  She rises through the haze.
Sainted Diana! can that be
  The Moon of Other Days?

Ah! shade of little Kitty Smith,
  Sweet Saint of Kensington!
Say, was it ever thus at Home
  The Moon of August shone,
When arm in arm we wandered long
  Through Putney's evening haze,
And Hammersmith was Heaven beneath
  The Moon of Other Days?

But Wandle's stream is Sutlej now,
  And Putney's evening haze

The dust that half a hundred kine
　　Before my window raise.
Unkempt, unclean, athwart the mist
　　The seething city looms,
In place of Putney's golden gorse
　　The sickly *babul* blooms.

Glare down, old Hecate, through the dust
　　And bid the pie-dog yell,
Draw from the drain its typhoid germ,
　　From each bazar its smell;
Yea, suck the fever from the tank
　　And sap my strength therewith:
Thank Heaven, you show a smiling face
　　To little Kitty Smith!

THE FALL OF JOCK GILLESPIE

This fell when dinner-time was done —
   'Twixt the first an' the second rub —
That oor mon Jock cam' hame again
   To his rooms ahint the Club.

An' syne he laughed, an' syne he sang,
   An' syne we thocht him fou,
An' syne he trumped his partner's trick,
   An' garred his partner rue.

Then up and spake an elder mon,
   That held the Spade its Ace —
"God save the lad!   Whence comes the licht
   "That wimples on his face?"

An' Jock he sniggered, an' Jock he smiled,
   An' ower the card-brim wunk:—
"I'm a' too fresh fra' the stirrup-peg,
   "May be that I am drunk."

"There's whusky brewed in Galashiels,
    "An' L. L. L. forbye;
"But never liquor lit the low
    "That keeks fra' oot your eye.

"There's a thrid o' hair on your dress-coat breast
    "Aboon the heart a wee?"
"Oh! that is fra' the lang-haired Skye
    "That slobbers ower me."

"Oh! lang-haired Skyes are lovin' beasts,
    "An' terrier dogs are fair,
"But never yet was terrier born,
    "Wi' ell-lang gowden hair!

"There's a smirch o' pouther on your breast
    "Below the left lappel?"
"Oh! that is fra' my auld cigar,
    "Whenas the stump-end fell."

"Mon Jock, ye smoke the Trichi coarse,
    "For ye are short o' cash.
"An' best Havannahs couldna leave,
    "Sae white an' pure an ash.

"This nicht ye stopped a story braid,
  "An' stopped it wi' a curse —
"Last nicht ye told that tale yoursel,
  "An' capped it wi' a worse!

"Oh! we're no fou!   Oh! we're no fou!
  "But plainly we can ken
"Ye're fallin', fallin', fra' the band
  "O' cantie single men!"

An' it fell when *sirris*-shaws were sere,
  An' the nichts were lang and mirk,
In braw new breeks, wi' a gowden ring,
  Oor Jockie gaed to the Kirk.

WHAT THE PEOPLE SAID

[JUNE 21ST, 1887]

By the well, where the bullocks go
Silent and blind and slow —
By the field, where the young corn dies
In the face of the sultry skies,
They have heard, as the dull Earth hears
The voice of the wind of an hour,
The sound of the Great Queen's voice:—
"My God hath given me years,
"Hath granted dominion and power:
"And I bid you, O Land, rejoice."

And the Ploughman settles the share
More deep in the grudging clod;
For he saith:—"The wheat is my care
"And the rest is the will of God.
"He sent the Mahratta spear
"As He sendeth the rain,
"And the *Mlech*, in the fated year,
"Broke the spear in twain,

"And was broken in turn.   Who knows
"How our Lords make strife?
"It is good that the young wheat grows,
"For the bread is Life."

Then, far and near, as the twilight drew,
    Hissed up to the scornful dark
Great serpents, blazing, of red and blue,
That rose and faded, and rose anew,
    That the Land might wonder and mark.
"To-day is a day of days," they said,
"Make merry, O People all!"
And the Ploughman listened and bowed his head:—
"To-day and to-morrow God's Will," he said,
As he trimmed the lamps on the wall.

"He sendeth us years that are good,
"As He sendeth the dearth.
"He giveth to each man his food,
"Or Her food to the Earth.
"Our Kings and our Queens are afar —
"On their peoples be peace —
"God bringeth the rain to the Bar,
"That our cattle increase."

And the Ploughman settled the share
More deep in the sun-dried clod:—
"Mogul, Mahratta, and *Mlech* from the North,
"And White Queen over the Seas —
"God raiseth them up and driveth them forth
"As the dust of the ploughshare flies in the breeze;
"But the wheat and the cattle are all my care,
"And the rest is the will of God."

THE UNDERTAKER'S HORSE

"To-tschin-shu is condemned to death. How can he drink tea with the executioner?" — JAPANESE PROVERB.

THE eldest son bestrides him,
And the pretty daughter rides him,
And I meet him oft o' mornings on the Course;
And there wakens in my bosom
An emotion chill and gruesome
As I canter past the Undertaker's Horse.

Neither shies he nor is restive,
But a hideously suggestive
Trot, professional and placid, he affects;
And the cadence of his hoof-beats
To my mind this grim reproof beats:—
"Mend your pace, my friend, I'm coming. Who's
    the next?"

Ah! stud-bred of ill-omen,
I have watched the strongest go — men

Of pith and might and muscle — at your heels,
Down the plantain-bordered highway
(Heaven send it ne'er be my way!),
In a lacquered box and jetty upon wheels.

Answer, sombre beast and dreary,
Where is Brown, the young, the cheery,
Smith, the pride of all his friends and half the Force?
You were at that last dread *dak*
We must cover at a walk,
Bring them back to me, O Undertaker's Horse!

With your mane unhogged and flowing,
And your curious way of going,
And that business-like black crimping of your tail,
E'en with Beauty on your back, Sir,
Pacing as a lady's hack, Sir,
What wonder when I meet you I turn pale?

It may be you wait your time, Beast,
Till I write my last bad rhyme, Beast,
Quit the sunlight, cut the rhyming, drop the glass,
Follow after with the others,
Where some dusky heathen smothers
Us with marigolds in lieu of English grass.

Or, perchance, in years to follow,
I shall watch your plump sides hollow,
See Carnifex (gone lame) become a corse,
See old age at last o'erpower you,
And the Station Pack devour you,
I shall chuckle then, O Undertaker's Horse!

But to insult, gibe, and quest, I've
Still the hideously suggestive
Trot that hammers out the unrelenting text,
And I hear it hard behind me
In what place soe'er I find me:—
"Sure to catch you sooner or later.   Who's the next?"

ONE VICEROY RESIGNS

So here's your Empire.   No more wine, then? Good.
We'll clear the Aides and *khitmatgars* away.
(You'll know that fat old fellow with the knife —
He keeps the Name Book, talks in English, too,
And almost thinks himself the Government.)
O Youth, Youth, Youth!   Forgive me, you're so
    young.
Forty from sixty — twenty years of work
And power to back the working.   *Ay de mi!*
You want to know, you want to see, to touch
And, by your lights, to act.   It's natural.
I wonder can I help you.   Let me try.
You saw — what did you see from Bombay east?
Enough to frighten any one but me?
Near that!   It frightened Me in Eighty-Four!
You shouldn't take a man from Canada
And bid him smoke in powder-magazines;
Nor with a Reputation such as . . .   Bah!
That ghost has haunted me for twenty years,

142

My Reputation now full-blown — Your fault —
Yours, with your stories of the strife at Home,
Who's up, who's down, who leads and who is led —
One reads so much, one hears so little here.
Well, now's your turn of exile.   I go back
To Rome and leisure.   All roads lead to Rome.
Or books — the refuge of the destitute.
When you . . . that brings me back to India.   See!
   Start clear.   *I* couldn't.   Egypt served my turn.
You'll never plumb the Oriental mind,
And if you did it isn't worth the toil.
Think of a sleek French priest in Canada;
Divide by twenty half-breeds.   Multiply
By twice the Sphinx's silence.   There's your East,
And you're as wise as ever.   So am I.

   Accept on trust and work in darkness, strike
At venture, stumble forward, make your mark,
(It's chalk on granite,) then thank God no flame
Leaps from the rock to shrivel mark and man.
I'm clear — my mark is made.   Three months of
     drouth
Had ruined much.   It rained and washed away
The specks that might have gathered on my Name.
I took a country twice the size of France,

And shuttered up one doorway in the North.
I stand by those.   You'll find that both will pay,
I pledged my Name on both — they're yours to-night.
Hold to them — they hold fame enough for two.
I'm old, but I shall live till Burma pays.
Men   there — *not*   German   traders — Cr-sthw-te
knows — You'll find it in my papers.   For the North
Guns always — quietly — but always guns.
You've seen your Council?   Yes, they'll try to rule,
And prize their Reputations.   Have you met
A grim lay-reader with a taste for coins,
And faith in Sin most men withhold from God?
He's gone to England.   R-p-n knew his grip
And kicked.   A Council always has its H-pes.
They look for nothing from the West but Death
Or Bath or Bournemouth.   Here's their ground.

                                        They fight
Until the middle classes take them back,
One of ten millions plus a C. S. I.
Or drop in harness.   Legion of the Lost?
Not altogether — earnest, narrow men,
But chiefly earnest, and they'll do your work,
And end by writing letters to the *Times*.
(Shall *I* write letters, answering H-nt-r — fawn

With R-p-n on the Yorkshire grocers?   Ugh!)
They have their Reputations.   Look to one —
I work with him — the smallest of them all,
White-haired, red-faced, who sat the plunging horse
Out in the garden.   He's your right-hand man,
And dreams of tilting W-ls-y from the throne,
But while he dreams gives work we cannot buy;
He has his Reputation — wants the Lords
By way of Frontier Roads.   Meantime, I think,
He values very much the hand that falls
Upon his shoulder at the Council table —
Hates cats and knows his business: *which is yours*.

　　Your business!   Twice a hundred million souls.
Your business!   I could tell you what I did
Some nights of Eighty-Five, at Simla, worth
A Kingdom's ransom.   When a big ship drives
God knows to what new reef, the man at the wheel
Prays with the passengers.   They lose their lives,
Or rescued go their way; but he's no man
To take his trick at the wheel again — that's worse
Than drowning.   Well, a galled Mashobra mule
(You'll see Mashobra) passed me on the Mall,
And I was — some fool's wife had ducked and bowed
To show the others I would stop and speak.

Then the mule fell — three galls, a hand-breadth each
Behind the withers.   Mrs. Whatsisname
Leers at the mule and me by turns, thweet thoul!
"How could they make him carry such a load!"
I saw — it isn't often I dream dreams —
More than the mule that minute — smoke and flame
From Simla to the haze below.   That's weak.
You're   younger.   You'll   dream   dreams   before
    you've done.
You've youth, that's one — good workmen — that
    means two
Fair chances in your favour.   Fate's the third.
I know what *I* did.   Do you ask me, "Preach?"
I answer by my past or else go back
To platitudes of rule — or take you thus
In confidence and say:—"You know the trick:
"You've governed Canada. You know. *You* know!"
And all the while commend you to Fate's hand
(Here at the top one loses sight o' God),
Commend you, then, to something more than you —
The Other People's blunders and . . . that's all.
I'd agonize to serve you if I could.
It's incommunicable, like the cast
That drops the tackle with the gut adry.

Too much — too little — there's your salmon lost!
And so I tell you nothing — wish you luck,
And wonder — how I wonder! — for your sake
And triumph for my own.   You're young, you're
    young,
You hold to half a hundred Shibboleths.
I'm old.   I followed Power to the last,
Gave her my best, and Power followed Me.
It's worth it — on my soul I'm speaking plain,
Here by the claret glasses! — worth it all.
I gave — no matter what I gave — I win.
I *know* I win.   Mine's work, good work that lives!
A country twice the size of France — the North
Safeguarded.   That's my record: sink the rest
And better if you can.   The Rains may serve,
Rupees may rise — three pence will give you Fame —
It's rash to hope for sixpence — If they rise
Get guns, more guns, and lift the salt-tax.

                                        Oh!

I told you what the Congress meant or thought?
I'll answer nothing.   Half a year will prove
The full extent of time and thought you'll spare
To Congress.   Ask a Lady Doctor *once*
How little Begums see the light — deduce

Thence how the True Reformer's child is born.

It's interesting, curious . . . and vile.

I told the Turk he was a gentleman.

I told the Russian that his Tartar veins

Bled pure Parisian ichor; and he purred.

The Congress doesn't purr.   I think it swears.

You're young — you'll swear too ere you've reached
    the end.

The End!   God help you, if there be a God.

(There must be one to startle Gl-dst-ne's soul

In that new land where all the wires are cut,

And Cr-ss snores anthems on the asphodel.)

God help you!   And I'd help you if I could,

But that's beyond me.   Yes, your speech was **crude**.

Sound claret after olives — yours and mine;

But Medoc slips into vin ordinaire.

(I'll drink my first at Genoa to your health)

Raise it to Hock.   You'll never catch my style.

And, after all, the middle-classes grip

The middle-class — for Brompton talk Earl's Court.

Perhaps you're right.   I'll see you in the *Times* —

A quarter-column of eye-searing print,

A leader once a quarter — then a war;

The Strand abellow through the fog:—"Defeat!"

" 'Orrible slaughter!"   While you lie awake
And wonder.   Oh, you'll wonder ere you're free!
I wonder now.   The four years slide away
So fast, so fast, and leave me here alone.
R—y C-lv-n, L—l, R-b-rts, B-ck, the rest,
Princes and Powers of Darkness, troops and trains,
(I *cannot* sleep in trains,) land piled on land,
Whitewash and weariness, red rockets, dust,
White snows that mocked me, palaces — with
    draughts,
And W-stl-nd with the drafts he couldn't pay,
Poor W-ls-n reading his obituary
Before he died, and H-pe, the man with bones,
And A-tch-s-n a dripping mackintosh
At Council in the Rains, his grating "Sirrr"
Half drowned by H-nt-r's silky:—"Bát my lahd."
Hunterian always: M-rsh-l spinning plates
Or standing on his head; the Rent Bill's roar,
A hundred thousand speeches, much red cloth,
And Smiths thrice happy if I call them Jones,
(I can't remember half their names) or reined
My pony on the Mall to greet their wives.
More trains, more troops, more dust, and then all's
    done.

Four years, and I forget.   If I forget
How will *they* bear me in their minds?   The North
Safeguarded — nearly (R-b-rts knows the rest),
A country twice the size of France annexed.
That stays at least.   The rest may pass — may pass—
Your heritage — and I can teach you naught.
"High trust," "vast honour," "interests twice as
    vast,"
"Due reverence to your Council"— keep to those.
I envy you the twenty years you've gained,
But not the five to follow.   What's that?   One!
Two!— Surely not so late.   Good-night.   *Don'*
    dream.

THE GALLEY-SLAVE

Oh gallant was our galley from her carven steering
    wheel
To her figurehead of silver and her beak of ham-
    mered steel;
The leg-bar chafed the ankle and we gasped for
    cooler air,
But no galley on the water with our galley could
    compare!

Our bulkheads bulged with cotton and our masts
    were stepped in gold —
We ran a mighty merchandise of niggers in the hold;
The white foam spun behind us, and the black
    shark swam below,
As we gripped the kicking sweep-head and we made
    that galley go.

'Twas merry in the galley, for we revelled now and
    then —
If they wore us down like cattle, faith, we fought and
    loved like men!

As we snatched her through the water, so we
    snatched a minute's bliss,
And the mutter of the dying never spoiled the lovers'
    kiss.

Our women and our children toiled beside us in the
    dark —
They died, we filed their fetters, and we heaved
    them to the shark —
We heaved them to the fishes, but so fast the galley
    sped
We had only time to envy, for we could not mourn
    our dead.

Bear witness, once my comrades, what a hard-bit
    gang were we —
The servants of the sweep-head but the masters of
    the sea!
By the hands that drove her forward as she plunged
    and yawed and sheered,
Woman, Man, or God or Devil, was there anything
    we feared?

Was it storm? Our fathers faced it and a wilder
    never blew;

Earth that waited for the wreckage watched the
    galley struggle through.
Burning noon or choking midnight, Sickness, Sorrow,
    Parting, Death?
Nay, our very babes would mock you had they time
    for idle breath.

But to-day I leave the galley and another takes my
    place;
There's my name upon the deck-beam — let it stand
    a little space.
I am free — to watch my messmates beating out to
    open main
Free of all that Life can offer — save to handle sweep
    again.

By the brand upon my shoulder, by the gall of
    clinging steel,
By the welt the whips have left me, by the scars that
    never heal;
By eyes grown old with staring through the sun-
    wash on the brine,
I am paid in full for service — would that service
    still were mine!

Yet they talk of times and seasons and of woe the
    years bring forth,
Of our galley swamped and shattered in the rollers of
    the North.
When the niggers break the hatches and the decks
    are gay with gore.
And a craven-hearted pilot crams her crashing on
    the shore.

She will need no half-mast signal, minute-gun, or
    rocket-flare,
When the cry for help goes seaward, she will find her
    servants there.
Battered chain-gangs of the orlop, grizzled drafts of
    years gone by,
To the bench that broke their manhood, they shall
    lash themselves and die.

Hale and crippled, young and aged, paid, deserted,
    shipped away —
Palace, cot, and lazaretto shall make up the tale
    that day
When the skies are black above them, and the decks
    ablaze beneath,
And the top-men clear the raffle with their clasp-
    knives in their teeth.

It may be that Fate will give me life and leave to
    row once more —
Set some strong man free for fighting as I take awhile
    his oar.
But to-day I leave the galley. Shall I curse her
    service then?
God be thanked — whate'er comes after, I have
    lived and toiled with Men!

A TALE OF TWO CITIES

WHERE the sober-coloured cultivator smiles
    On his *byles;*
Where the cholera, the cyclone, and the Crow
    Come and go;
Where the merchant deals in indigo and tea,
    Hides and *ghi;*
Where the Babu drops inflammatory hints
    In his prints;
Stands a City — Charnock chose it — packed away
    Near a Bay —
By the sewage rendered fetid, by the sewer
    Made impure,
By the Sunderbunds unwholesome, by the swamp
    Moist and damp;
And the City and the Viceroy, as we see,
    Don't agree.

Once, two hundred years ago, the trader came
    Meek and tame.

Where his timid foot first halted, there he stayed,
   Till mere trade
Grew to Empire, and he sent his armies forth
   South and North.
Till the country from Peshawar to Ceylon
   Was his own.
Thus the midday halt of Charnock — more's the pity!
   Grew a City.
As the fungus sprouts chaotic from its bed,
   So it spread —
Chance-directed, chance-erected, laid and built
   On the silt —
Palace, byre, hovel — poverty and pride —
   Side by Side;
And, above the packed and pestilential town,
   Death looked down.

But the Rulers in that City by the Sea,
   Turned to flee —
Fled, with each returning Spring-tide from its ills
   To the Hills.
From the clammy fogs of morning, from the blaze
   Of the days,
From the sickness of the noontide, from the heat
   Beat retreat;

For the country from Peshawar to Ceylon
        Was their own.
But the Merchant risked the perils of the Plain
        For his gain.
Now the resting-place of Charnock, 'neath the palms,
        Asks an alms,
And the burden of its lamentation is,
        Briefly, this:—
"Because, for certain months, we boil and stew,
        "So should you.
"Cast the Viceroy and his Council, to perspire
        "In our fire!"
And for answer to the argument, in vain
        We explain
That an amateur Saint Lawrence cannot cry:—
        "*All* must fry!"
That the Merchant risks the perils of the Plain
        For his gain.
Nor can Rulers rule a house that men grow rich in,
        From its kitchen.

Let the Babu drop inflammatory hints
        In his prints;
And mature — consistent soul — his plan for stealing
        To Darjeeling:

Let the Merchant seek, who makes his silver pile,
      England's isle;
Let the City Charnock pitched on — evil day!—
      Go Her way.
Though the argosies of Asia at Her doors
      Heap their stores,
Though Her enterprise and energy secure
      Income sure,
Though "out-station orders punctually obeyed"
      Swell Her trade —
Still, for rule, administration, and the rest
      Simla's best.

IN SPRINGTIME

My garden blazes brightly with the rose-bush and
    the peach,
  And the *köil* sings above it, in the *siris* by the well,
From the creeper-covered trellis comes the squirrel's
    chattering speech,
  And the blue jay screams and flutters where the
    cheery *satbhai* dwell.

But the rose has lost its fragrance, and the *köil's*
    note is strange;
  I am sick of endless sunshine, sick of blossom-
    burdened bough.
Give me back the leafless woodlands where the winds
    of Springtime range —
  Give me back one day in England, for it's Spring
    in England now!

Through the pines the gusts are booming, o'er the
    brown fields blowing chill,
  From the furrow of the plough-share streams the
    fragrance of the loam,

And the hawk nests in the cliffside and the jackdaw
    on the hill,
  And my heart is back in England 'mid the sights
    and sounds of Home.
But the garland of the sacrifice this wealth of rose
    and peach is,
  Ah! *köïl*, little *köïl*, singing on the *siris* bough,
In my ears the knell of exile your ceaseless bell-like
    speech is —
  Can you tell me aught of England or of Spring in
    England now?

GIFFEN'S DEBT

Imprim is he was "broke." Thereafter left
His regiment and, later, took to drink;
Then, having lost the balance of his friends,
"Went Fantee"— joined the people of the land,
Turned three parts Mussulman and one Hindu,
And lived among the Gauri villagers,
Who gave him shelter and a wife or twain,
And boasted that a thorough, full-blood *sahib*
Had come among them. Thus he spent his time,
Deeply indebted to the village *shroff*,
(Who never asked for payment always drunk,
Unclean, abominable, out-at-heels;
Forgetting that he was an Englishman.

You know they dammed the Gauri with a dam,
And all the good contractors scamped their work,
And all the bad material at hand
Was used to dam the Gauri — which was cheap,
And, therefore, proper. Then the Gauri burst,
And several hundred thousand cubic tons

Of water dropped into the valley, *flop*,
And drowned some five and twenty villagers,
And did a lakh or two of detriment
To crops and cattle.   When the flood went down
We found him dead, beneath an old dead horse,
Full six miles down the valley.   So we said
He was a victim to the Demon Drink,
And moralized upon him for week,
And then forgot him.   Which was natural.

But, in the valley of the Gauri, men
Beneath the shadow of the big new dam,
Relate a foolish legend of the flood,
Accounting for the little loss of life
(Only those five and twenty villagers)
In this wise:— On the evening of the flood,
They heard the groaning of the rotten dam,
And voices of the Mountain Devils.   Then
An incarnation of the local God,
Mounted upon a monster-neighing horse,
And flourishing a flail-like whip, came down,
Breathing ambrosia, to the villages,
And fell upon the simple villagers
With yells beyond the power of mortal throat,
And blows beyond the power of mortal hand,

And smote them with the flail-like whip, and drove
Them clamorous with terror up the hill,
And scattered, with the monster-neighing steed,
Their crazy cottages about their ears,
And generally cleared those villages.
Then came the water, and the local God,
Breathing ambrosia, flourishing his whip,
And mounted on his monster-neighing steed,
Went down the valley with the flying trees
And residue of homesteads, while they watched
Safe on the mountain-side these wondrous things,
And knew that they were much beloved of Heaven.

Wherefore, and when the dam was newly built,
They raised a temple to the local God,
And burnt all manner of unsavoury things
Upon his altar, and created priests,
And blew into a conch and banged a bell,
And told the story of the Gauri flood
With circumstance and much embroidery.

So be, the whiskified Objectionable,
Unclean, abominable, out-at-heels,
Became the tutelary Deity
Of all the Gauri valley villages;
And may in time become a Solar Myth.

TWO MONTHS

In June

No hope, no change!   The clouds have shut us in,
  And through the cloud the sullen Sun strikes down
  Full on the bosom of the tortured Town.
Till Night falls heavy as remembered sin
That will not suffer sleep or thought of ease.
  And, hour on hour, the dry-eyed Moon in spite
  Glares through the haze and mocks with watery
    light
The torment of the uncomplaining trees.
Far off, the Thunder bellows her despair
To echoing Earth thrice parched.   The lightnings fly
In vain.   No help the heaped-up clouds afford,
But wearier weight of burdened, burning air.
What truce with Dawn?   Look, from the aching sky
Day stalks, a tyrant with a flaming sword!

TWO MONTHS

In September

At dawn there was a murmur in the trees,
  A ripple on the tank, and in the air
  Presage of coming coolness — everywhere
A voice of prophecy upon the breeze.
Up leapt the Sun and smote the dust to gold,
  And strove to parch anew the heedless land,
All impotently, as a King grown old
  Wars for the Empire crumbling 'neath his hand.

One after one, the lotos-petals fell,
Beneath the onslaught of the rebel year
In mutiny against a furious sky;
And far-off Winter whispered: —"It is well!
"Hot Summer dies.   Behold your help is near,
"For when men's need is sorest, then come I."

L'ENVOI

To whom it may concern

THE smoke upon your Altar dies,
  The flowers decay,
The Goddess of your sacrifice
  Has flown away.
What profit then to sing or slay
The sacrifice from day to day?

"We know the Shrine is void," they said,
  "The Goddess flown —
"Yet wreaths are on the altar laid —
  "The Altar-Stone
"Is black with fumes of sacrifice,
"Albeit She has fled our eyes.

"For, it may be, if still we sing
  "And tend the Shrine,
"Some Deity on wandering wing
  "May there incline;
"And, finding all in order meet,
"Stay while we worship at Her feet."

BALLADS

AND

BARRACK-ROOM BALLADS

*Beyond the path of the outmost sun, through utter darkness
hurled,*
Further than ever comet flared or vagrant star-dust swirled,
*Sit such as fought and sailed and ruled and loved and made our
world.*

*They are purged of pride because they died; they know the
worth of their bays;*
*They sit at wine with the Maidens Nine, and the Gods of the
Elder Days —*
It is their will to serve or be still as fitteth our Father's praise.

*'Tis theirs to sweep through the ringing deep where Azrael's
outposts are,*
*Or buffet a path through the Pit's red wrath when God goes out
to war,*
*Or hang with the reckless Seraphim on the rein of a redmaned
star.*

*They take their mirth in the joy of the earth — they dare not
grieve for her pain —*
*For they know of toil and the end of toil — they know God's
Law is plain;*
*So they whistle the Devil to make them sport who know that sin
is vain.*

*And ofttimes cometh our wise Lord God, master of every
trade,*
*And tells them tales of the Seventh Day — of Edens newly
made,*
*And they rise to their feet as He passes by — gentlemen un-
afraid.*

To these who are cleansed of base Desire, Sorrow and Lust
    and Shame —
Gods, for they knew the heart of Men — men, for they stooped
    to Fame —
Borne on the breath that men call Death, my brother's spirit
    came.

Scarce had he need to cast his pride or slough the dross of
    earth.
E'en as he trod that day to God, so walked he from his
    birth —
In simpleness and gentleness and honour and clean mirth.

So, cup to lip in fellowship, they gave him welcome high
And made him place at the banquet board, the Strong Men
    ranged thereby,
Who had done his work and held his peace and had no fear
    to die.

Beyond the loom of the last lone star through open darkness
    hurled,
Further than rebel comet dared or living star-swarm swirled,
Sits he with such as praise our God for that they served his
    world.

PREFACE

The greater part of the "Barrack-Room Ballads," as well as "Cleared," "Tomlinson," and "The English Flag," have appeared in the "National Observer." Messrs. Macmillan and Co. have kindly given me permission to reproduce four ballads contributed to their Magazine, And I am indebted to the "St. James Gazette" for a like courtesy in regard to the ballads of the "Clampherdown" and "Bolivar," and the "Imperial Rescript." "The Ryhme of the Three Captains" was printed first in the "Athenæum." I fancy that most of the other verses are new.

RUDYARD KIPLING.

BALLADS

THE BALLAD OF EAST AND WEST

Oh, East is East, and West is West, and never the
    twain shall meet,
Till Earth and Sky stand presently at God's great
    Judgment Seat;
But there is neither East nor West, Border, nor Breed,
    nor Birth,
When two strong men stand face to face, tho' they come
    from the ends of the earth!

Kamal is out with twenty men to raise the Border
    side,
And he has lifted the Colonel's mare that is the
    Colonel's pride:
He has lifted her out of the stable-door between the
    dawn and the day,
And turned the calkins upon her feet, and ridden
    her far away.

Then up and spoke the Colonel's son that led a
    troop of the Guides:

"Is there never a man of all my men can say where
    Kamal hides?"

Then up and spoke Mahommed Khan, the son of
    the Ressaldar,

"If ye know the track of the morning-mist, ye know
    where his pickets are.

"At dusk he harries the Abazai — at dawn he is into
    Bonair,

"But he must go by Fort Bukloh to his own place to
    fare,

"So if ye gallop to Fort Bukloh as fast as a bird can
    fly,

"By the favour of God ye may cut him off ere he
    win to the Tongue of Jagai,

"But if he be passed the Tongue of Jagai, right
    swiftly turn ye then,

"For the length and the breadth of that grisly plain
    is sown with Kamal's men.

"There is rock to the left, and rock to the right, and
    low lean thorn between,

"And ye may hear a breech-bolt snick where never a
    man is seen."

The Colonel's son has taken a horse, and a raw
    rough dun was he,

With the mouth of a bell and the heart of Hell,
    and the head of the gallows-tree.

The Colonel's son to the Fort has won, they bid
    him stay to eat —

Who rides at the tail of a Border thief, he sits not
    long at his meat.

He's up and away from Fort Bukloh as fast as he
    can fly,

Till he was aware of his father's mare in the gut of
    the Tongue of Jagai,

Till he was aware of his father's mare with Kamal
    upon her back,

And when he could spy the white of her eye, he
    made the pistol crack.

He has fired once, he has fired twice, but the whist-
    ling ball went wide.

"Ye shoot like a soldier," Kamal said. "Show now
    if ye can ride."

It's up and over the Tongue of Jagai, as blown dust-
    devils go,

The dun he fled like a stag of ten, but the mare like
    a barren doe.

The dun he leaned against the bit and slugged his
    head above,
But the red mare played with the snaffle-bars, as a
    maiden plays with a glove.
There was rock to the left and rock to the right,
    and low lean thorn between,
And thrice he heard a breech-bolt snick tho' never
    a man was seen.

They have ridden the low moon out of the sky, their
    hoofs drum up the dawn,
The dun he went like a wounded bull, but the mare
    like a new-roused fawn.
The dun he fell at a water-course — in a woeful heap
    fell he,
And Kamal has turned the red mare back, and
    pulled the rider free.

He has knocked the pistol out of his hand — small
    room was there to strive,
"'Twas only by favour of mine," quoth he, "ye rode
    so long alive:
"There was not a rock for twenty mile, there was
    not a clump of tree,
"But covered a man of my own men with his rifle
    cocked on his knee.

"If I had raised my bridle-hand, as I have held
it low,

"The little jackals that flee so fast, were feasting all
in a row:

"If I had bowed my head on my breast, as I have
held it high,

"The kite that whistles above us now were gorged
till she could not fly."

Lightly answered the Colonel's son:—"Do good to
bird and beast,

"But count who come for the broken meats before
thou makest a feast.

"If there should follow a thousand swords to carry
my bones away,

"Belike the price of a jackal's meal were more than
a thief could pay.

"They will feed their horse on the standing crop,
their men on the garnered grain,

"The thatch of the byres will serve their fires when
all the cattle are slain.

"But if thou thinkest the price be fair,— thy
brethren wait to sup,

"The hound is kin to the jackal-spawn,— howl, dog,
and call them up!

"And if thou thinkest the price be high, in steer
and gear and stack,

"Give me my father's mare again, and I'll fight my
own way back!"

Kamal has gripped him by the hand and set him
upon his feet.

"No talk shall be of dogs," said he, "when wolf and
grey wolf meet.

"May I eat dirt if thou hast hurt of me in deed or
breath;

"What dam of lances brought thee forth to jest at
the dawn with Death?"

Lightly answered the Colonel's son: "I hold by the
blood of my clan:

"Take up the mare for my father' sgift — by God,
she has carried a man!"

The red mare ran to the Colonel's son, and nuzzled
against his breast,

"We be two strong men," said Kamal then, "but she
loveth the younger best.

"So she shall go with a lifter's dower, my turquoise-
studded rein,

"My broidered saddle and saddle-cloth, and silver
stirrups twain."

The Colonel's son a pistol drew and held it muzzle-
    end,

"Ye have taken the one from a foe," said he; "will
    ye take the mate from a friend?"

"A gift for a gift," said Kamal straight; "a limb for
    the risk of a limb.

"Thy father has sent his son to me, I'll send my
    son to him!"

With that he whistled his only son, that dropped
    from a mountain-crest —

He trod the ling like a buck in spring, and he
    looked like a lance in rest.

"Now here is thy master," Kamal said, "who leads a
    troop of the Guides,

"And thou must ride at his left side as shield on
    shoulder rides.

"Till Death or I cut loose the tie, at camp and
    board and bed,

"Thy life is his — thy fate it is to guard him with
    thy head.

"So thou must eat the White Queen's meat, and all
    her foes are thine,

"And thou must harry thy father's hold for the
    peace of the Border-line,

"And thou must make a trooper tough and hack thy
    way to power —
"Belike they will raise thee to Ressaldar when I am
    hanged in Peshawur."

They have looked each other between the eyes, and
    there they found no fault,
They have taken the Oath of the Brother-in-Blood
    on leavened bread and salt:
They have taken the Oath of the Brother-in-Blood
    on fire and fresh-cut sod,
On the hilt and the haft of the Khyber knife, and
    the Wondrous Names of God.
The Colonel's son he rides the mare and Kamal's
    boy the dun,
And two have come back to Fort Bukloh where
    there went forth but one.
And when they drew to the Quarter-Guard, full
    twenty swords flew clear —
There was not a man but carried his feud with the
    blood of the mountaineer.
"Ha' done! ha' done!" said the Colonel's son.
    "Put up the steel at your sides!

Last night ye had struck at a Border thief — to-
night 'tis a man of the Guides!"

Oh, East is East and West is West, and never the two
shall meet,
Till Earth and Sky stand presently at God's great
Judgment Seat;
But there is neither East nor West, Border, nor Breed,
nor Birth,
When two strong men stand face to face, tho' they come
from the ends of the earth.

THE LAST SUTTEE

Not many years ago a King died in one of the Rajpoot States. His wives, disregarding the orders of the English against suttee, would have broken out of the palace had not the gates been barred. But one of them, disguised as the King's favourite dancing-girl, passed through the line of guards and reached the pyre. There, her courage failing, she prayed her cousin, a baron of the court, to kill her. This he did, not knowing who she was.

UDAI CHAND lay sick to death
    In his hold by Gungra hill.
All night we heard the death-gongs ring
For the soul of the dying Rajpoot King,
All night beat up from the women's wing
    A cry that we could not still.

All night the barons came and went,
    The lords of the outer guard:
All night the cressets glimmered pale
On Ulwar sabre and Tonk jezail,
Mewar headstall and Marwar mail,
    That clinked in the palace yard.

12

In the Golden room on the palace roof
 All night he fought for air:
And there was sobbing behind the screen,
Rustle and whisper of women unseen,
And the hungry eyes of the Boondi Queen
 On the death she might not share.

He passed at dawn — the death-fire leaped
 From ridge to river-head,
From the Malwa plains to the Abu scaurs
And wail upon wail went up to the stars
Behind the grim zenana-bars,
 When they knew that the King was dead

The dumb priest knelt to tie his mouth
 And robe him for the pyre.
The Boondi Queen beneath us cried:
"See, now, that we die as our mothers died
"In the bridal-bed by our master's side!
 "Out, women!— to the fire!"

We drove the great gates home apace:
 White hands were on the sill:

But ere the rush of the unseen feet
Had reached the turn to the open street,
The bars shot down, the guard-drum beat —
  We held the dove-cot still.

A face looked down in the gathering day,
  And laughing spoke from the wall:
"Ohé, they mourn here: let me by —
"Azizun, the Lucknow nautch-girl, I?
"When the house is rotten, the rats must fly,
  "And I seek another thrall.

"For I ruled the King as ne'er did Queen,—
  "To-night the Queens rule me!
"Guard them safely, but let me go,
"Or ever they pay the debt they owe
"In scourge and torture!"   She leaped below,
  And the grim guard watched her flee.

They knew that the King had spent his soul
  On a North-bred dancing girl:
That he prayed to a flat-nosed Lucknow god,
And kissed the ground where her feet had trod,
And doomed to death at her drunken nod
  And swore by her lightest curl.

We bore the King to his fathers' place,
    Where the tombs of the Sun-born stand:
Where the grey apes swing, and the peacocks preen
On fretted pillar and jewelled screen,
And the wild boar couch in the house of the
        Queen
    On the drift of the desert sand.

The herald read his titles forth,
    We set the logs aglow:
"Friend of the English, free from fear,
"Baron of Luni to Jeysulmeer,
"Lord of the Desert of Bikaneer,
    "King of the Jungle,— go!"

All night the red flame stabbed the sky
    With wavering wind-tossed spears:
And out of a shattered temple crept
A woman who veiled her head and wept,
And called on the King — but the great King slept,
    And turned not for her tears.

Small thought had he to mark the strife —
    Cold fear with hot desire —

When thrice she leaped from the leaping flame
And thrice she beat her breast for shame
And thrice like a wounded dove she came
    And moaned about the fire

One watched, a bow-shot from the blaze,
    The silent streets between,
Who had stood by the King in sport and fray,
To blade in ambush or boar at bay,
And he was a baron old and grey,
    And kin to the Boondi Queen.

He said: "O shameless, put aside
    "The veil upon thy brow!
"Who held the King and all his land
"To the wanton will of a harlot's hand!
"Will the white ash rise from the blistered brand?
    "Stoop down, and call him now!"

Then she: "By the faith of my tarnished soul,
    "All things I did not well
"I had hoped to clear ere the fire died,
"And lay me down by my master's side
To rule in Heaven his only bride,
    "While the others howl in Hell.

"But I have felt the fire's breath,
    "And hard it is to die!
"Yet if I may pray a Rajpoot lord
"To sully the steel of a Thakur's sword
"With base-born blood of a trade abhorred,"—
    And the Thakur answered, "Ay."

He drew and struck: the straight blade drank
    The life beneath the breast.
"I had looked for the Queen to face the flame,
"But the harlot dies for the Rajpoot dame —
"Sister of mine, pass, free from shame.
    "Pass with thy King to rest!"

The black log crashed above the white:
    The little flames and lean,
Red as slaughter and blue as steel,
That whistled and fluttered from head to heel,
Leaped up anew, for they found their meal
    On the heart of — the Boondi Queen!

THE BALLAD OF THE KING'S MERCY

*Abdhur Rahman, the Durani Chief, of him is the
    story told.*
*His mercy fills the Khyber hills — his grace is
    manifold;*
*He has taken toll of the North and the South — his
    glory reacheth far,*
*And they tell the tale of his charity from Balkh to
    Kandahar.*

Before the old Peshawur Gate, where Kurd and
    Kaffir meet,
The Governor of Kabul dealt the Justice of the
    Street,
And that was strait as running noose and swift as
    plunging knife,
Tho' he who held the longer purse might hold the
    longer life.

There was a hound of Hindustan had struck a
    Euzufzai,
Wherefore they spat upon his face and led him out
    to die.
It chanced the King went forth that hour when
    throat was bared to knife;
The Kaffir grovelled under-hoof and clamoured for
    his life.

Then said the King: "Have hope, O friend! Yea,
    Death disgraced is hard;
"Much honour shall be thine"; and called the Captain
    of the Guard,
Yar Khan, a bastard of the Blood, so city-babble
    saith,
And he was honoured of the King — the which is
    salt to Death;
And he was son of Daoud Shah the Reiver of the
    Plains,
And blood of old Durani Lords ran fire in his
    veins;
And 'twas to tame an Afghan pride nor Hell nor
    Heaven could bind,
The King would make him butcher to a yelping cur
    of Hind.

"Strike!" said the King.   "King's blood art thou—
    his death shall be his pride!"
Then louder, that the crowd might catch: "Fear
    not — his arms are tied!"
Yar Khan drew clear the Khyber knife, and struck,
    and sheathed again.
"O man, thy will is done," quoth he; "A King this
    dog hath slain."

    Abdhur Rahman, the Durani Chief, to the North
        and the South is sold.
    The North and the South shall open their mouth to
        a Ghilzai flag unrolled,
    When the big guns speak to the Khyber peak, and
        his dog-Heratis fly,
    Ye have heard the song — How long?   How long?
        Wolves of the Abazai!

That night before the watch was set, when all the
    streets were clear,
The Governor of Kabul spoke: 'My King, hast thou
    no fear?
"Thou knowest—thou hast heard,"—his speech died
    at his masters' face.

And grimly said the Afghan King: "I rule the
   Afghan race.
"My path is mine — see thou to thine — to-night
   upon thy bed
"Think who there be in Kabul now that clamour for
   thy head."

That night when all the gates were shut to City and
   to Throne,
Within a little garden-house the King lay down
   alone.
Before the sinking of the moon, which is the Night
   of Night,
Yar Khan came softly to the King to make his
   honour white.
The children of the town had mocked beneath his
   horse's hoofs,
The harlots of the town had hailed him "butcher!"
   from their roofs.
But as he groped against the wall, two hands upon
   him fell,
The King behind his shoulder spoke: "Dead man,
   thou dost not well!

"'Tis ill to jest with Kings by day and seek a boon
   by night;
"And that thou bearest in thy hand is all too sharp
   to write.
"But three days hence, if God be good, and if thy
   strength remain,
"Thou shalt demand one boon of me and bless me
   in thy pain.
"For I am merciful to all, and most of all to thee.
"My butcher of the shambles, rest — no knife hast
   thou for me!"

*Abdhur Rahman, the Durani Chief, holds hard by
   the South and the North;*
*But the Ghilzai knows, ere the melting snows, when
   the swollen banks break forth,*
*When the red-coats crawl to the sungar wall, and
   his Usbeg lances fail.*
*Ye have heard the song —How long?   How long?
   Wolves of the Zuka Kheyl!*

They stoned him in the rubbish-field when dawn
   was in the sky,
According to the written word, "See that he do not
   die."

They stoned him till the stones were piled above
    him on the plain,
And those the labouring limbs displaced they
    tumbled back again.

One watched beside the dreary mound that veiled
    the battered thing,
And him the King with laughter called the Herald
    of the King.

It was upon the second night, the night of Ramazan,
The watcher leaning earthward heard the message
    of Yar Kkan.
From shattered breast through shrivelled lips broke
    forth the rattling breath:
"Creature of God, deliver me from agony of Death."

They sought the King among his girls, and risked
    their lives thereby:
"Protector of the Pitiful, give orders that he die!"

"Bid him endure until the day," a lagging answer
    came;
"The night is short, and he can pray and learn to
    bless my name."

Before the dawn three times he spoke, and on
    the day once more:
"Creature of God, deliver me and bless the King
    therefore!"

They shot him at the morning prayer, to ease him
    of his pain,
And when he heard the matchlocks clink, he blessed
    the King again.
Which thing the singers made a song for all the
    world to sing,
So that the Outer Seas may know the mercy of the
    King.

*Abdhur Rahman, the Durani Chief, of him is the
    story told.*
*He has opened his mouth to the North and the
    South, they have stuffed his mouth with gold.*
*Ye know the truth of his tender ruth — and sweet
    his favours are.*
*Ye have heard the song — How long? How long?
    from Balkh to Kandahar.*

THE BALLAD OF THE KING'S JEST

WHEN spring-time flushes the desert grass,
Our kafilas wind through the Khyber Pass.
Lean are the camels but fat the frails,
Light are the purses but heavy the bales,
As the snowbound trade of the North comes down
To the market-square of Peshawur town.

In a turquoise twilight, crisp and chill,
A kafila camped at the foot of the hill.
Then blue smoke-haze of the cooking rose,
And tentpeg answered to hammer-nose;
And the picketed ponies shag and wild,
Strained at their ropes as the feed was piled;
And the bubbling camels beside the load
Sprawled for a furlong adown the road;
And the Persian pussy-cats, brought for sale,
Spat at the dogs from the camel-bale;
And the tribesmen bellowed to hasten the food;

And the camp-fires twinkled by Fort Jumrood;
And there fled on the wings of the gathering dusk
A savour of camels and carpets and musk,
A murmur of voices, a reek of smoke,
To tell us the trade of the Khyber woke.

The lid of the flesh-pot chattered high,
The knives were whetted and — then came I
To Mahbub Ali, the muleteer,
Patching his bridles and counting his gear,
Crammed with the gossip of half a year.
But Mahbub Ali the kindly said,
"Better is speech when the belly is fed."
So we plunged the hand to the mid-wrist deep
In a cinnamon stew of the fat-tailed sheep,
And he who never hath tasted the food,
By Allah! he knoweth not bad from good.

We cleansed our beards of the mutton-grease,
We lay on the mats and were filled with peace,
And the talk slid north, and the talk slid south,
With the sliding puffs from the hookah-mouth
Four things greater than all things are,—
Women and Horses and Power and War.
We spake of them all, but the last the most,

For I sought a word of a Russian post.
Of a shifty promise, an unsheathed sword
And a grey-coat guard on the Helmund ford.
Then Mahbub Ali lowered his eyes
In the fashion of one who is weaving lies.
Quoth he: "Of the Russians who can say?
"When the night is gathering all is grey.
"But we look that the gloom of the night shall die
"In the morning flush of a blood-red sky.
"Friend of my heart, is it meet or wise
"To warn a King of his enemies?
"We know what Heaven or Hell may bring,
"But no man knoweth the mind of the King.
"That unsought counsel is cursed of God
"Attesteth the story of Wali Dad.

"His sire was leaky of tongue and pen,
"His dam was a clucking Khuttuck hen;
"And the colt bred close to the vice of each,
"For he carried the curse of an unstaunched speech.
"Therewith madness — so that he sought
"The favour of kings at the Kabul court;
"And travelled, in hope of honour, far
"To the line where the grey-coat squadrons are.
"There have I journeyed too — but I

"Saw naught, said naught, and — did not die!
"He hearked to rumour, and snatched at a breath
"Of 'this one knoweth' and 'that one saith,'—
"Legends that ran from mouth to mouth
"Of a grey-coat coming, and sack of the South.
"These have I also heard — they pass
"With each new spring and the winter grass.

"Hot-foot southward, forgotten of God,
"Back to the city ran Wali Dad,
"Even to Kabul — in full durbar
"The King held talk with his Chief in War.
"Into the press of the crowd he broke,
"And what he had heard of the coming spoke.

"Then Gholam Hyder, the Red Chief, smiled,
"As a mother might on a babbling child;
"But those who would laugh restrained their breath,
"When the face of the King showed dark as death.
"Evil it is in full durbar
"To cry to a ruler of gathering war!
"Slowly he led to a peach-tree small,
"That grew by a cleft of the city wall.
"And he said to the boy: 'They shall praise thy zeal
" 'So long as the red spurt follows the steel.

"'And the Russ is upon us even now?
"'Great is thy prudence — await them, thou.
"'Watch from the tree.   Thou art young and strong,
"'Surely thy vigil is not for long.
"'The Russ is upon us, thy clamour ran?
"'Surely an hour shall bring their van.
"'Wait and watch.   When the host is near,
"'Shout aloud that my men may hear.'

"Friend of my heart, is it meet or wise
"To warn a King of his enemies?
"A guard was set that he might not flee —
"A score of bayonets ringed the tree.
"The peach-bloom fell in showers of snow,
"When he shook at his death as he looked below.
"By the power of God, who alone is great,
"Till the seventh day he fought with his fate.
"Then madness took him, and men declare
"He mowed in the branches as ape and bear,
"And last as a sloth, ere his body failed,
"And he hung as a bat in the forks, and wailed,
"And sleep the cord of his hands untied,
"And he fell, and was caught on the points and died.

"Heart of my heart, is it meet or wise
"To warn a King of his enemies?

"We know what Heaven or Hell may bring,
"But no man knoweth the mind of the King.
"Of the grey-coat coming who can say?
"When the night is gathering all is grey.
"Two things greater than all things are,
"The first is Love, and the second War.
"And since we know not how War may prove,
"Heart of my heart, let us talk of Love!"

WITH SCINDIA TO DELHI

More than a hundred years ago, in a great battle fought near Delhi, an Indian Prince rode fifty miles after the day was lost with a beggar-girl, who had loved him and followed him in all his camps, on his saddle bow. He lost the girl when almost within sight of safety. A Maratta trooper tells the story:—

THE wreath of banquet overnight lay withered on
    the neck,
  Our hands and scarves were saffron-dyed for
      signal of despair,
When we went forth to Paniput to battle with the
    Mlech,—
  Ere we came back from Paniput and left a king-
      dom there.

Thrice thirty-thousand men were we to force the
    Jumna fords —
  The hawk-winged horse of Damajee, mailed
      squadrons of the Bhao,

Stark levies of the southern hills, the Deccan's
    sharpest swords,
  And he the harlot's traitor son the goatherd
    Mulhar Rao!

Thrice thirty-thousand men were we before the mists
    had cleared,
  The low white mists of morning heard the war-
    conch scream and bray;
We called upon Bhowani and we gripped them by
    the beard,
  We rolled them like a flood and washed their
    ranks away.

The children of the hills of Khost before our lances
    ran,
  We drove the black Rohillas back as cattle to the
    pen;
'Twas then we needed Mulhar Rao to end what we
    began,
  A thousand men had saved the charge; he fled
    the field with ten!

There was no room to clear a sword — no power to
    strike a blow,
  For foot to foot, ay, breast to breast, the battle
    held us fast —
Save where the naked hill men ran and stabbing
    from below
  Brought down the horse and rider and we trampled
    them and passed.

To left the roar of musketry rang like a falling
    flood —
  To right the sunshine rippled red from redder
    lance and blade —
Above the dark *Upsaras*[1] flew, beneath us plashed
    the blood,
  And, bellying black against the dust, the Bhagwa
    Jhanda swayed.

I saw it fall in smoke and fire, the banner of the
    Bhao;
  I heard a voice across the press of one who called
    in vain:—

[1] The Choosers of the Slain

"Ho! Anand Rao Nimbalkhur ride! Get aid of
   Mulhar Rao!
  "Go shame his squadrons into fight — the Bhao —
      the Bhao is slain!"

Thereat, as when a sand-bar breaks in clotted
   spume and spray —
   When rain of later autumn sweeps the Jumna
      water-head,
Before their charge from flank to flank our riven
   ranks gave way;
   But of the waters of that flood the Jumna fords
      ran red.

I held by Scindia, my lord, as close as man might
   hold;
   A Soobah of the Deccan asks no aid to guard his
      life;
But Holkar's Horse were flying, and our chiefest
   chiefs were cold,
   And like a flame among us leapt the long lean
      Northern knife.

I held by Scindia — my lance from butt to tuft was
    dyed,
  The froth of battle bossed the shield and roped
    the bridle-chain —
What time beneath our horses' feet a maiden rose
    and cried,
  And clung to Scindia, and I turned a sword-cut
    from the twain.

(He set a spell upon the maid in woodlands long
    ago,
  A hunter by the Tapti banks she gave him water
    there:
He turned her heart to water, and she followed to
    her woe.
  What need had he of Lalun who had twenty maids
    as fair?)

Now in that hour strength left my lord; he wrenched
    his mare aside;
  He bound the girl behind him and we slashed and
    struggled free.

Across the reeling wreck of strife we rode as shadows
    ride
  From Paniput to Delhi town, but not alone
    were we.

'Twas Lutuf-Ullah Populzai laid horse upon our
    track,
  A swine-fed reiver of the North that lusted for the
    maid;
I might have barred his path awhile, but Scindia
    called me back,
  And I — Oh woe for Scindia!— I listened and
    obeyed.

League after league the formless scrub took shape
    and glided by —
  League after league the white road swirled behind
    the white mare's feet —
League after league, when leagues were done, we
    heard the Populzai,
  Where sure as Time and swift as Death the tireless
    footfall beat.

Noon's eye beheld that shame of flight, the shadows
    fell, we fled
  Where steadfast as the wheeling kite he followed
    in our train;
The black wolf warred where we had warred, the
    jackal mocked our dead,
  And terror born of twilight tide made mad the
    labouring brain.

I gasped:—"A kingdom waits my lord; her love
    is but her own.
  'A day shall mar, a day shall cure for her, but what
    for thee?
"Cut loose the girl: he follows fast.   Cut loose and
    ride alone!"
  Then Scindia 'twixt his blistered lips:—"My
    Queen's Queen shall she be!

"Of all who eat my bread last night 'twas she alone
    that came
  "To seek her love between the spears and find her
    crown therein!

"One shame is mine to-day, what need the weight of
  double shame?
  "If once we reach the Delhi gate, though all be
    lost, I win! "

We rode — the white mare failed — her trot a
  staggering stumble grew,—
  The cooking-smoke of even rose and weltered
    and hung low;
And still we heard the Populzai and still we strained
  anew,
  And Delhi town was very near, but nearer was
    the foe.

Yea, Delhi town was very near when Lalun whis-
  pered: —"Slay!
  "Lord of my life, the mare sinks fast — stab deep
    and let me die!"
But Scindia would not, and the maid tore free and
  flung away,
  And turning as she fell we heard the clattering
    Populzai.

Then Scindia checked the gasping mare that rocked
    and groaned for breath,
  And wheeled to charge and plunged the knife a
    hands-breadth in her side —
The hunter and the hunted know how that last pause
    is death —
  The blood had chilled about her heart, she reared
    and fell and died.

Our Gods were kind.   Before he heard the maiden's
    piteous scream
  A log upon the Delhi road, beneath the mare he
    lay —
Lost mistress and lost battle passed before him like
    a dream;
  The darkness closed about his eyes — I bore my
    King away.

THE BALLAD OF BOH DA THONE

This is the ballad of Boh Da Thone,
Erst a Pretender to Theebaw's throne,
Who harried the district of Alalone:
How he met with his fate and the V.P.P.
At the hand of Harendra Mukerji,
Senior Gomashta, G.B.T.

Boh Da Thone was a warrior bold,
His sword and his Snider were bossed with gold,

And the Peacock Banner his henchman bore
Was stiff with bullion but stiffer with gore.

He shot at the strong and he slashed at the weak
From the Salween scrub to the Chindwin teak:

He crucified noble, he sacrificed mean,
He filled old women with kerosene:

While over the water the papers cried,
"The patriot fights for his countryside!"

40

But little they cared for the Native Press,
The worn white soldiers in Khaki dress,

Who tramped through the jungle and camped in the
    byre,
Who died in the swamp and were tombed in the
    mire,

Who gave up their lives, at the Queen's Command,
For the Pride of their Race and the Peace of the
    Land.

Now, first of the foemen of Boh Da Thone
Was Captain O'Neil of the "Black Tyrone,"

And his was a Company, seventy strong,
Who hustled that dissolute Chief along.

There were lads from Galway and Louth and
    Meath
Who went to their death with a joke in their teeth,

And worshipped with fluency, fervour, and zeal
The mud on the boot-heels of "Crook" O'Neil.

But ever a blight on their labours lay,
And ever their quarry would vanish away,

Till the sun-dried boys of the Black Tyrone
Took a brotherly interest in Boh Da Thone:

And, sooth, if pursuit in possession ends,
The Boh and his trackers were best of friends.

The word of a scout — a march by night —
A rush through the moist — a scattering fight —

A volley from cover — a corpse in the clearing —
The glimpse of a loin-cloth and heavy jade earring —

The flare of a village — the tally of slain —
And . . . the Boh was abroad "on the raid" again!

They cursed their luck as the Irish will,
They gave him credit for cunning and skill,

They buried their dead, they bolted their beef,
And started anew on the track of the thief

Till, in place of the "Kalends of Greece," men said,
"When Crook and his darlings come back with
    the head."

They had hunted the Boh from the Hills to the
    plain —
He doubled and broke for the hills again:

They had crippled his power for rapine and raid,
They had routed him out of his pet stockade,

And at last, they came, when the Day Star tired,
To a camp deserted — a village fired.

A black cross blistered the Morning-gold,
And the body upon it was stark and cold.

The wind of the dawn went merrily past,
The high grass bowed her plumes to the blast.

And out of the grass, on a sudden, broke
A spirtle of fire, a whorl of smoke —

And Captain O'Neil of the Black Tyrone
Was blessed with a slug in the ulna-bone —
The gift of his enemy Boh Da Thone.

(Now a slug that is hammered from telegraph-wire
Is a thorn in the flesh and a rankling fire.)

. . . .

The shot-wound festered — as shot-wounds may
In a steaming barrack at Mandalay.

The left arm throbbed, and the Captain swore,
"I'd like to be after the Boh once more!"

The fever held him — the Captain said,
"I'd give a hundred to look at his head!"

The Hospital punkahs creaked and whirred,
But Babu Harendra (Gomashta) heard.

He thought of the cane-brake, green and dank,
That girdled his home by the Dacca tank.

He thought of his wife and his High School son,
He thought — but abandoned the thought—of a gun.

His sleep was broken by visions dread
Of a shining Boh with a silver head.

He kept his counsel and went his way,
And swindled the cartmen of half their pay.

. . . .

And the months went on, as the worst must do,
And the Boh returned to the raid anew.

But the Captain had quitted the long-drawn strife,
And in far Simoorie had taken a wife.

And she was a damsel of delicate mould,
With hair like the sunshine and heart of gold,

And little she knew the arms that embraced
Had cloven a man from the brow to the waist:

And little she knew that the loving lips
Had ordered a quivering life's eclipse,

And the eye that lit at her lightest breath
Had glared unawed in the Gates of Death.

(For these be matters a man would hide,
As a general rule, from an innocent Bride.)

And little the Captain thought of the past,
And, of all men, Babu Harendra last.

.   .   .   .

But slow, in the sludge of the Kathun road,
The Government Bullock Train toted its load.

Speckless and spotless and shining with *ghee*,
In the rearmost cart sat the Babu-jee.

And ever a phantom before him fled
Of a scowling Boh with a silver head.

Then the lead-cart stuck, though the coolies slaved,
And the cartmen flogged and the escort raved;

And out of the jungle, with yells and squeals,
Pranced Boh Da Thone, and his gang at his heels!

Then belching blunderbuss answered back
The Snider's snarl and the carbine's crack,

And the blithe revolver began to sing
To the blade that twanged on the locking-ring,

And the brown flesh blued where the bay'net
    kissed,
As the steel shot back with a wrench and a twist,

And the great white bullocks with onyx eyes
Watched the souls of the dead arise,

And over the smoke of the fusillade
The Peacock Banner staggered and swayed.

Oh, gayest of scrimmages man may see
Is a well-worked rush on the G.B.T.!

The Babu shook at the horrible sight,
And girded his ponderous loins for flight,

But Fate had ordained that the Boh should start
On a lone-hand raid of the rearmost cart,

And out of that cart, with a bellow of woe,
The Babu fell — flat on the top of the Boh!

For years had Harendra served the State,
To the growth of his purse and the girth of his
    pêt —

There were twenty stone, as the tally-man knows,
On the broad of the chest of this best of Bohs.

And twenty stone from a height discharged
Are bad for a Boh with a spleen enlarged.

Oh, short was the struggle — severe was the shock —
He dropped like a bullock — he lay like a block;

And the Babu above him, convulsed with fear,
Heard the labouring life-breath hissed out in his
    ear.

And thus in a fashion undignified
The princely pest of the Chindwin died.

.   .   .   .

Turn now to Simoorie where, lapped in his ease,
The Captain is petting the Bride on his knees,

Where the *whit* of the bullet, the wounded man's
  scream
Are mixed as the mist of some devilish dream —

Forgotten, forgotten the sweat of the shambles
Where the hill-daisy blooms and the grey monkey
  gambols,

From the sword-belt set free and released from the
  steel,
The Peace of the Lord is with Captain O'Neil.

Up the hill to Simoorie — most patient of drudges —
The bags on his shoulder, the mail-runner trudges.

"For Captain O'Neil, *Sahib*.   One hundred and ten
Rupees to collect on delivery."

                                          Then
(Their breakfast was stopped while the screw-jack
  and hammer
Tore wax-cloth, split teak-wood, and chipped out
  the dammer;)

Open-eyed, open-mouthed, on the napery's snow,
With a crash and a thud, rolled — the Head of the
  Boh!

And gummed to the scalp was a letter which
    ran:—

              "IN FIELDING FORCE SERVICE.

                  "*Encampment,*

                      "10th Jan.

"Dear Sir,— I have honour to send, *as you said,*
"For final approval (see under) Boh's Head;

"Was took by myself in most bloody affair.
"By High Education brought pressure to bear.

"Now violate Liberty, time being bad,
"To mail V.P.P. (rupees hundred) Please add

"Whatever Your Honour can pass.   Price of Blood
"Much cheap at one hundred, and children want
    food.

"So trusting Your Honour will somewhat retain
"True love and affection for Govt. Bullock Train,

"And show awful kindness to satisfy me,
        "I am,
            "Graceful Master,
                "Your
                      "H. Mukerji."

As the rabbit is drawn to the rattlesnake's power,
As the smoker's eye fills at the opium hour,

As a horse reaches up to the manger above,
As the waiting ear yearns for the whisper of love,

From the arms of the Bride, iron-visaged and slow,
The Captain bent down to the Head of the Boh.

And e'en as he looked on the Thing where It lay
'Twixt the winking new spoons and the napkins'
        array,

The freed mind fled back to the long-ago days —
The hand-to-hand scuffle — the smoke and the
        blaze —

The forced march at night and the quick rush at
        dawn —
The banjo at twilight, the burial ere morn —

The stench of the marshes — the raw, piercing smell
When the overhand stabbing-cut silenced the yell —

The oaths of his Irish that surged when they stood
Where the black crosses hung o'er the Kuttamow
        flood.

As a derelict ship drfits away with the tide
The Captain went out on the Past from his Bride,

Back, back, through the springs to the chill of the
    year,
When he hunted the Boh from Maloon to Tsaleer.

As the shape of a corpse dimmers up through deep
    water,
In his eye lit the passionless passion of slaughter,

And men who had fought with O'Neil for the life
Had gazed on his face with less dread than his wife.

For she who had held him so long could not hold
    him —
Though a four-month Eternity should have con-
    trolled him —

But watched the twin Terror — the head turned to
    head —
The scowling, scarred Black, and the flushed savage
    Red —

The spirit that changed from her knowing and flew
    to
Some grim hidden Past she had never a clue to,

But It knew as It grinned, for he touched it un-
    fearing,
And muttered aloud, "So you kept that jade ear-
    ring!"

Then nodded, and kindly, as friend nods to friend,
"Old man, you fought well, but you lost in the end."

.   .   .   .

The visions departed, and Shame followed Passion
"He took what I said in this horrible fashion,

"*I'll* write to Harendra!"   With language unsainted
The Captain came back to the Bride who had
    fainted.

.   .   .   .

And this is a fiction?   No.   Go to Simoorie
And look at their baby, a twelve-month old Houri,

A pert little, Irish-eyed Kathleen Mavournin —
She's always about on the Mall of a mornin'—

And you'll see, if her right shoulder-strap is dis-
    placed,
This: *Gules* upon *argent*, a Boh's Head, *erased!*

THE LAMENT OF THE BORDER CATTLE THIEF

O WOE is me for the merry life
  I led beyond the Bar,
And a treble woe for my winsome wife
  That weeps at Shalimar.

They have taken away my long jezail,
  My shield and sabre fine,
And heaved me into the Central Jail
  For lifting of the kine.

The steer may low within the byre,
  The Jut may tend his grain,
But there'll be neither loot nor fire
  Till I come back again.

And God have mercy on the Jut
  When once my fetters fall,
And Heaven defend the farmer's hut
  When I am loosed from thrall.

It's woe to bend the stubborn back
  Above the grinching quern,
It's woe to hear the leg-bar clack
  And jingle when I turn!

But for the sorrow and the shame,
  The brand on me and mine,
I'll pay you back in leaping flame
  And loss of the butchered kine.

For every cow I spared before
  In charity set free,
If I may reach my hold once more
  I'll reive an honest three!

For every time I raised the low
  That scared the dusty plain,
By sword and cord, by torch and tow
  I'll light the land with twain!

Ride hard, ride hard to Abazai,
  Young *Sahib* with the yellow hair —
Lie close, lie close as khuttucks lie,
  Fat herds below Bonair!

The one I'll shoot at twilight tide,
   At dawn I'll drive the other;
The black shall mourn for hoof and hide,
   The white man for his brother!

'Tis war, red war, I'll give you then,
   War till my sinews fail,
For the wrong you have done to a chief of men
   And a thief of the Zukka Kheyl.

And if I fall to your hand afresh
   I give you leave for the sin,
That you cram my throat with the foul pig's
      flesh
And swing me in the skin!

THE RHYME OF THE THREE CAPTAINS

This ballad appears to refer to one of the exploits of the notorious Paul Jones, the Amercian Pirate.   It is founded on fact.

        . . . At the close of a winter day,
Their anchors down, by London town the Three
        Great Captains lay.
And one was Admiral of the North from Solway
        Firth to Skye,
And one was Lord of the Wessex coast and all the
        lands thereby,
And one was Master of the Thames from Limehouse
        to Blackwall.
And he was Captain of the Fleet — the bravest of
        them all.
Their good guns guarded their great grey sides that
        were thirty foot in the sheer,
When there came a certain trading-brig with news
        of a privateer.

Her rigging was rough with the clotted drift that
    drives in a Northern breeze,

Her sides were clogged with the lazy weed that
    spawns in the Eastern seas.

Light she rode in the rude tide-rip, to left and right
    she rolled,

And the skipper sat on the scuttle-butt and stared
    at an empty hold.

"I ha' paid Port dues for your Law," quoth he, "and
    where is the Lawyer boast

"If I sail unscathed from a heathen port to be
    robbed on a Christian coast?

"Ye have smoked the hives of the Laccadives as we
    burn the lice in a bunk;

"We tack not now to a Gallang prow or a plunging
    Pei-ho junk;

"I had no fear but the seas were clear as far as a sail
    might fare

"Till I met with a lime-washed Yankee brig that
    rode off Finisterre.

"There were canvas blinds to his bow-gun ports to
    screen the weight he bore

"And the signals ran for a merchantman from Sandy
    Hook to the Nore.

"He would not fly the Rovers' flag — the bloody or
    the black,

"But now he floated the Gridiron and now he
    flaunted the Jack.

"He spoke of the Law as he crimped my crew — he
    swore it was only a loan;

"But when I would ask for my own again, he swore
    it was none of my own.

"He has taken my little parrakeets that nest beneath
    the Line,

"He has stripped my rails of the shaddock-frails and
    the green unripened pine;

"He has taken my bale of dammer and spice I won
    beyond the seas,

"He has taken my grinning heathen gods — and what
    should he want o' these?

"My foremast would not mend his boom, my deck-
    house patch his boats;

"He has whittled the two this Yank Yahoo, to peddle
    for shoepeg-oats.

"I could not fight for the failing light and a rough
    beam-sea beside,

"But I hulled him once for a clumsy crimp and twice
    because he lied.

The skipper called to the tall taffrail: "And what
     is that to me?

"Did ever you hear of a privateer that rifled a
     Seventy-three?

"Do I loom so large from your quarter-deck that I
     lift like a ship o' the Line?

"He has learned to run from a shotted gun and harry
     such craft as mine.

"There is never a Law on the Cocos Keys to hold
     a white man in,

"But we do not steal the niggers' meal, for that is a
     nigger's sin.

"Must he have his Law as a quid to chaw, or laid in
     brass on his wheel?

"Does he steal with tears when he buccaneers?
     Fore Gad, then, why does he steal?"

The skipper bit on a deep-sea word, and the word it
     was not sweet,

For he could see the Captains Three had signalled
     to the Fleet.

But three and two, in white and blue, the whimper-
     ing flags began:

"We have heard a tale of a foreign sail, but he is a
     merchantman."

The skipper peered beneath his palm and swore by
    the Great Horn Spoon,

''Fore Gad, the Chaplain of the Fleet would bless
    my picaroon!''

By two and three the flags blew free to lash the
    laughing air,

"We have sold our spars to the merchantman — we
    know that his price is fair."

The skipper winked his Western eye, and swore by
    a China storm:—

"They ha' rigged him a Joseph's jury-coat to keep
    his honour warm."

The halliards twanged against the tops, the bunting
    bellied broad,

The skipper spat in the empty hold and mourned
    for a wasted cord.

Masthead — masthead, the signal sped by the line
    o' the British craft;

The skipper called to his Lascar crew, and put her
    about and laughed:—

"It's mainsail haul, my bully boys all — we'll out to
    the seas again;

"Ere they set us to paint their pirate saint, or scrub
    at his grapnel-chain

"It's fore-sheet free, with her head to the sea, and
the swing of the unbought brine —

"We'll make no sport in an English court till we
come as a ship o' the Line,

"Till we come as a ship o' the Line, my lads, of
thirty foot in the sheer,

"Lifting again from the outer main with news of a
privateer;

"Flying his pluck at our mizzen-truck for weft of
Admiralty,

"Heaving his head for our dipsy-lead in sign that we
keep the sea.

"Then fore-sheet home as she lifts to the foam — we
stand on the outward tack

"We are paid in the coin of the white man's trade —
the bezant is hard, ay, and black.

"The frigate-bird shall carry my word to the Kling
and the Orang-Laut

"How a man may sail from a heathen coast to be
robbed in a Christian port;

"How a man may be robbed in Christian port while
Three Great Captains there

"Shall dip their flag to a slaver's rag — to show that
his trade is fair!"

THE BALLAD OF THE "CLAMPHERDOWN"

I⊤ was our war-ship "Clampherdown"
  Would sweep the Channel clean,
Wherefore she kept her hatches close
When the merry Channel chops arose,
  To save the bleached marine.

She had one bow-gun of a hundred ton,
  And a great stern-gun beside;
They dipped their noses deep in the sea,
They racked their stays and staunchions free
  In the wash of the wind-whipped tide.

It was our war-ship "Clampherdown,"
  Fell in with a cruiser light
That carried the dainty Hotchkiss gun
And a pair o' heels wherewith to run,
  From the grip of a close-fought fight.

She opened fire at seven miles —
　　As ye shoot at a bobbing cork —
And once she fired and twice she fired,
Till the bow-gun dropped like a lily tired
　　That lolls upon the stalk.

"Captain, the bow-gun melts apace,
　　"The deck-beams break below,
"'Twere well to rest for an hour or twain,
"And botch the shattered plates again."
　　And he answered, "Make it so."

She opened fire within the mile —
　　As ye shoot at the flying duck —
And the great stern-gun shot fair and true.
With the heave of the ship, to the stainless
　　　blue,
　　And the great stern-turret stuck.

"Captain, the turret fills with steam,
　　"The feed-pipes burst below —
"You can hear the hiss of helpless ram,
"You can hear the twisted runners jam."
　　And he answered, "Turn and go!"

It was our war-ship "Clampherdown,"
  And grimly did she roll;
Swung round to take the cruiser's fire
As the White Whale faces the Thresher's ire,
  When they war by the frozen Pole.

"Captain, the shells are falling fast,
  "And faster still fall we;
"And it is not meet for English stock,
"To bide in the heart of an eight-day clock,
  "The death they cannot see."

"Lie down, lie down my bold A.B.,
  "We drift upon her beam;
"We dare not ram for she can run;
"And dare ye fire another gun,
  "And die in the peeling steam?"

It was our war-ship "Clampherdown"
  That carried an armour-belt;
But fifty feet at stern and bow,
Lay bare as the paunch of the purser's sow,
  To the hail of the Nordenfeldt.

"Captain, they lack us through and through;
   "The chilled steel bolts are swift!
"We have emptied the bunkers in open sea,
"Their shrapnel bursts where our coal should be."
   And he answered, "Let her drift."

It was our war-ship "Clampherdown,"
   Swung round upon the tide,
Her two dumb guns glared south and north,
And the blood and the bubbling steam ran forth,
   And she ground the cruiser's side.

"Captain, they cry, the fight is done,
   "They bid you send your sword."
And he answered, "Grapple her stern and bow.
"They have asked for the steel. They shall have
     it now;
   "Out cutlasses and board!"

It was our war-ship "Clampherdown,"
   Spewed up four hundred men;
And the scalded stokers yelped delight,
As they rolled in the waist and heard the fight,
   Stamp o'er their steel-walled pen.

They cleared the cruiser end to end,
   From conning-tower to hold.
They fought as they fought in Nelson's fleet;
They were stripped to the waist, they were bare
      to the feet,
   As it was in the days of old.

It was the sinking 'Clampherdown"
   Heaved up her battered side —
And carried a million pounds in steel,
To the cod and the corpse-fed conger-eel
   And the scour of the Channel tide.

It was the crew of the "Clampherdown"
   Stood out to sweep the sea,
On a cruiser won from an ancient foe.
As it was in the days of long-ago,
   And as it still shall be.

THE BALLAD OF THE "BOLIVAR"

Seven men from all the world, back to Docks again,
Rolling down the Ratcliffe Road drunk and raising
    Cain:
Give the girls another drink 'fore we sign away —
We that took the "Bolivar" out across the Bay!

We put out from Sunderland loaded down with
    rails;
  We put back to Sunderland 'cause our cargo
    shifted;
We put out from Sunderland — met the winter
    gales —
  Seven days and seven nights to the Start we
    drifted.

    Racketing her rivets loose, smoke-stack white
      as snow,
    All the coals adrift a deck, half the rails below

Leaking like a lobster-pot, steering like a
dray —
Out we took the "Bolivar," out across the Bay!

One by one the Lights came up, winked and let us
by;
Mile by mile we waddled on, coal and fo'c'sle
short;
Met a blow that laid us down, heard a bulkhead
fly;
Left The Wolf behind us with a two foot-list to
port.

Trailing like a wounded duck, working out her
soul;
Clanging like a smithy-shop after every roll;
Just a funnel and a mast lurching through the
spray —
So we threshed the "Bolivar" out across the
Bay!

Felt her hog and felt her sag, betted when she'd
break;
Wondered every time she raced if she'd stand the
shock;

Heard the seas like drunken men pounding at her
strake;
Hoped the Lord 'ud keep his thumb on the
plummer-block.

Banged against the iron decks, bilges choked
with coal;
Flayed and frozen foot and hand, sick of heart
and soul;
'Last we prayed she'd buck herself into Judgment Day —
Hi! we cursed the "Bolivar" knocking round
the Bay!

Oh! her nose flung up to sky, groaning to be still —
Up and down and back we went, never time for
breath;
Then the money paid at Lloyd's caught her by the
heel,
And the stars ran round and round dancin' at our
death.

Aching for an hour's sleep, dozing off between;
Heard the rotten rivets draw when she took it
green,

Watched the compass chase its tail like a cat at
play —
That was on the "Bolivar," south across the
Bay.

Once we saw between the squalls, lyin' head to
swell —
Mad with work and weariness, wishin' they was
we —
Some damned Liner's lights go by like a grand
hotel;
Cheered her from the "Bolivar," swampin' in
the sea.

Then a greyback cleared us out, then the
skipper laughed;
"Boys, the wheel has gone to Hell — rig the
winches aft!
"Yoke the kicking rudder-head — get her under
way!"
So we steered her, pulley-haul, out across the
Bay!"

Just a pack o' rotten plates puttied up with tar,
In we came, an' time enough 'cross Bilbao Bar.

Overloaded, undermanned, meant to founder,
  we
Euchred God Almighty's storm, bluffed the
  Eternal Sea!

Seven men from all the world, back to town again,
Rollin' down the Ratcliffe Road drunk and raising
  Cain.
Seven men from out of Hell.   Ain't the owners gay,
'Cause we took the "Bolivar" safe across the Bay?

THE LOST LEGION

THERE's a Legion that never was 'listed,
   That carries no colours or crest,
But, split in a thousand detachments,
   Is breaking the road for the rest.
Our fathers they left us their blessing —
   They taught us, and groomed us, and crammed;
But we've shaken the Clubs and the Messes
   To go and find out and be damned,
               Dear boys!
   To go and get shot and be damned.

So some of us chevy the slaver,
   And some of us cherish the black,
And some of us hunt on the Oil Coast,
   And some on — the Wallaby track:
And some of us drift to Sarawak,
   And some of us drift up The Fly,
And some share our tucker with tigers,
   And some with the gentle Masai,
               Dear boys!
   Take tea with the giddy Masai.

Copyright, 1893, by Macmillan & Co.

We've painted The Islands vermillion,
   We've pearled on half-shares in the Bay,
We've shouted on seven-ounce nuggets,
   We've starved on a Kanaka's pay.
We've laughed at the world as we found it,—
   Its women and cities and men —
From Say Yid Burgash in a tantrum
   To the smoke-reddened eyes of Loben,
              Dear boys!
   We've a little account with Loben.

We opened the Chinaman's oil-well,
   But the dynamite didn't agree,
And the people got up and *fan-kwaied* us,
   And we ran from Ichang to the sea.
Yes, somehow and somewhere and always
   We were first when the trouble began,
From a lottery-row in Manila
   To an I. D. B. race on the Pan,
              Dear boys!
   With the Mounted Police on the Pan.

We preach in advance of the Army,
   We skirmish ahead of the Church,
With never a gunboat to help us
   When we're scuppered and left in the lurch.

But we know as the cartridges finish
 And we're filed on our last little shelves,
That the Legion that never was 'listed
 Will send us as good as ourselves,
      (Good men!)
 Five hundred as good as ourselves.

Then a health (we must drink it in whispers),
 To our wholly unauthorised horde —
To the line of our dusty foreloopers,
 The Gentlemen Rovers abroad.
Yes, a health to ourselves ere we scatter,
 For the steamer won't wait for the train,
And the Legion that never was 'listed
 Goes back into quarters again.
     'Regards!
 Goes back under canvas again.
     Hurrah!
 The swag and the billy again.
     Here's how!
 The trail and the packhorse again.
     Salue!
 The trek and the lager again.

THE SACRIFICE OF ER-HEB

Er-Heb beyond the Hills of Ao-Safai
Bears witness to the truth, and Ao-Safai
Hath told the men of Gorukh.   Thence the tale
Comes westward o'er the peaks to India.

The story of Bisesa, Armod's child,—
A maiden plighted to the Chief in War
The Man of Sixty Spears who held the Pass
That leads to Thibet, but to-day is gone
To seek his comfort of the God called Budh
The Silent — showing how the Sickness ceased
Because of her who died to save the tribe.

Taman is One and greater than us all,
Taman is One and greater than all Gods:
Taman is Two in One and rides the sky,
Curved like a stallion's croup, from dusk to dawn,
And drums upon it with his heels, whereby
Is bred the neighing thunder in the hills.

This is Taman, the God of all Er-Heb,
Who was before all Gods, and made all Gods,
And presently will break the Gods he made,
And step upon the Earth to govern men
Who give him milk-dry ewes and cheat his
    Priests,
Or leave his shrine unlighted — as Er-Heb
Left it unlighted and forgot Taman,
When all the Valley followed after Kysh
And Yabosh, little Gods but very wise,
And from the sky Taman beheld their sin.

He sent the Sickness out upon the hills
The Red Horse Sickness with the iron hooves,
To turn the Valley to Taman again.

And the Red Horse snuffed thrice into the wind,
The naked wind that had no fear of him;
And the Red Horse stamped thrice upon the snow,
The naked snow that had no fear of him;
And the Red Horse went out across the rocks
The ringing rocks that had no fear of him;
And downward, where the lean birch meets the
    snow

And downward, where the grey pine meets the birch,
And downward, where the dwarf oak meets the pine,
Till at his feet our cup-like pastures lay.

That night, the slow mists of the evening dropped,
Dropped as a cloth upon a dead man's face,
And weltered in the valley, bluish-white
Like water very silent — spread abroad,
Like water very silent, from the Shrine
Unlighted of Taman to where the stream
Is dammed to fill our cattle-troughs — sent up
White waves that rocked and heaved and then were
    still,
Till all the Valley glittered like a marsh,
Beneath the moonlight, filled with sluggish mist
Knee-deep, so that men waded as they walked.

That night, the Red Horse grazed above the Dam
Beyond the cattle-troughs.   Men heard him feed,
And those that heard him sickened where they lay

Thus came the sickness to Er-Heb, and slew
Ten men, strong men, and of the women four;
And the Red Horse went hillward with the dawn,
But near the cattle-troughs his hoof-prints lay.

That night, the slow mists of the evening dropped,
Dropped as a cloth upon the dead, but rose
A little higher, to a young girl's height;
Till all the valley glittered like a lake,
Beneath the moonlight, filled with sluggish mist.

That night, the Red Horse grazed beyond the Dam
A stone's throw from the troughs.   Men heard him
 feed,
And those that heard him sickened where they lay
Thus came the sickness to Er-Heb, and slew
Of men a score, and of the women eight,
And of the children two.

       Because the road
To Gorukh was a road of enemies,
And Ao-Safai was blocked with early snow,
We could not flee from out the Valley.   Death
Smote at us in a slaughter-pen, and Kysh
Was mute as Yabosh, though the goats were slain;
And the Red Horse grazed nightly by the stream,
And later, outward, towards the Unlighted Shrine,
And those that heard him sickened where they
 lay.

Then said Bisesa to the Priests at dusk,
When the white mist rose up breast-high and choked
The voices in the houses of the dead:—
"Yabosh and Kysh avail not.   If the Horse
"Reach the Unlighted Shrine we surely die.
"Ye have forgotten of all Gods the Chief
"Taman!" Here rolled the thunder through the Hill.
And Yabosh shook upon his pedestal.
"Ye have forgotten of all Gods the chief
"Too long."   And all were dumb save one who cried
On Yabosh with the Sapphire 'twixt His knees
But found no answer in the smoky roof
And, being smitten of the sickness died
Before the altar of the Sapphire Shrine.

Then said Bisesa:—"I am near to Death,
"And have the Wisdom of the Grave for gift
"To bear me on the path my feet must tread.
"If there be wealth on earth, then I am rich,
"For Armod is the first of all Er-Heb;
"If there be beauty on the earth,"— her eyes
Dropped for a moment to the temple floor,—
"Ye know that I am fair.   If there be Love,
"Ye know that love is mine."   The Chief in War,

The Man of Sixty Spears, broke from the press,
And would have clasped her, but the Priests with-
  stood,
Saying:—"She has a message from Taman."
Then said Bisesa:—"By my wealth and love
"And beauty, I am chosen of the God
"Taman." Here rolled the thunder through the
  Hills
And Kysh fell forward on the Mound of Skulls.

In darkness and before our Priests, the maid
Between the altars, cast her bracelets down,
Therewith the heavy earrings Armod made,
When he was young, out of the water-gold
Of Gorukh — threw the breast-plate thick with jade
Upon the turquoise anklets — put aside
The bands of silver on her brow and neck;
And as the trinkets tinkled on the stones,
The Thunder of Taman lowed like a bull.

Then said Bisesa stretching out her hands,
As one in darkness fearing Devils:—"Help!
"O Priests, I am a woman very weak.

"And who am I to know the will of Gods?
"Taman hath called me — whither shall I go?"
The Chief in War, the Man of Sixty Spears
Howled in his torment fettered by the Priests
But dared not come to her to drag her forth,
And dared not lift his spear against the Priests.
Then all men wept.

                    There was a Priest of Kysh
Bent with a hundred winters, hairless, blind
And taloned as the great Snow-Eagle is.
His seat was nearest to the altar-fires,
And he was counted dumb among the Priests.
But, whether Kysh decreed, or from Taman
The impotent tongue found utterance we know
As little as the bats beneath the eaves.
He cried so that they heard who stood without: —
"To the Unlighted Shrine!" and crept aside
Into the shadow of his fallen God
And whimpered, and Bisesa went her away.

That night, the slow mists of the evening dropped,
Dropped as a cloth upon the dead, and rose
Above the roofs, and by the Unlighted Shrine

Lay as the slimy water of the troughs
When murrain thins the cattle of Er-Heb:
And through the mist men heard the Red Horse
    feed.

In Armod's house they burned Bisesa's dower,
And killed her black bull Tor, and broke her wheel,
And loosed her hair, as for the marriage-feast
With cries more loud than mourning for the dead.

Across the fields, from Armod's dwelling-place,
We heard Bisesa weeping where she passed
To seek the Unlighted Shrine; the Red Horse
    neighed
And followed her, and on the river-mint
His hooves struck dead and heavy in our ears.

Out of the mists of evening, as the star
Of Ao-Safai climbs through the black snow-blur
To show the Pass is clear, Bisesa stepped
Upon the great grey slope of mortised stone,
The Causeway of Taman.   The Red Horse neighed
Behind her to the Unlighed Shrine — then fled
North to the Mountain where his stable lies.

They know who dared the anger of Taman,
And watched that night above the clinging mists,
Far up the hill, Bisesa's passing in.

She set her hand upon the carven door,
Fouled by a myriad bats, and black with time,
Whereon is graved the Glory of Taman
In letters older than Ao-Safai;
And twice she turned aside and twice she wept,
Cast down upon the threshold, clamouring
For him she loved — the Man of Sixty Spears,
And for her father,— and the black bull Tor
Hers and her pride.   Yea, twice she turned away
Before the awful darkness of the door,
And the great horror of the Wall of Man
Where Man is made the plaything of Taman,
An Eyeless Face that waits above and laughs.

But the third time she cried and put her palms
Against the hewn stone leaves, and prayed Taman
To spare Er-Heb and take her life for price.

They know who watched, the doors were rent apart
And closed upon Bisesa, and the rain

Broke like a flood across the Valley, washed
The mist away; but louder than the rain
The thunder of Taman filled men with fear.

Some say that from the Unlighted Shrine she cried
For succour, very pitifully, thrice,
And others that she sang and had no fear.
And some that there was neither song nor cry,
But only thunder and the lashing rain.

Howbeit, in the morning, men rose up,
Perplexed with horror, crowding to the Shrine,
And when Er-Heb was gathered at the doors
The Priests made lamentation and passed in
To a strange Temple and a God they feared
But knew not.

            From the crevices the grass
Had thrust the altar-slabs apart, the walls
Were grey with stains unclean, the roof-beams
    swelled
With many-coloured growth of rottenness,
And lichen veiled the Image of Taman
In leprosy.   The Basin of the Blood

Above the altar held the morning sun
A winking ruby on its heart; below,
Face hid in hands, the maid Bisesa lay.

Er-Heb beyond the Hills of Ao-Safai
Bears witness to the truth, and Ao-Safai
Hath told the men of Gorukh.   Thence the tale
Comes westward o'er the peaks to India.

THE DOVE OF DACCA

THE freed dove flew to the Rajah's tower —
  Fled from the slaughter of Moslem kings —
And the thorns have covered the city of Gaur.
  Dove — dove — oh, homing dove!
Little white traitor, with woe on thy wings!

The Rajah of Dacca rode under the wall;
  He set in his bosom a dove of flight —
"If she return, be sure that I fall."
  Dove — dove — oh, homing dove!
Pressed to his heart in the thick of the fight.

"Fire the palace, the fort, and the keep —
  Leave to the foeman no spoil at all.
In the flame of the palace lie down and sleep
  If the dove, if the dove — if the homing dove
Come and alone to the palace wall."

The Kings of the North they were scattered abroad —
  The Rajah of Dacca he slew them all.
Hot from slaughter he stopped at the ford,
  And the dove — the dove — oh, the homing dove!
She thought of her cote on the palace wall.

She opened her wings and she flew away —
  Fluttered away beyond recall;
She came to the palace at break of day.
  Dove — dove — oh, homing dove!
Flying so fast for a kingdom's fall.

The Queens of Dacca they slept in flame —
  Slept in the flame of the palace old —
To save their honour from Moslem shame.
  And the dove — the dove — oh, the homing dove!
She cooed to her young where the smoke-cloud rolled.

The Rajah of Dacca rode far and fleet,
  Followed as fast as a horse could fly,
He came and the palace was black at his feet;
  And the dove — the dove — the homing dove,
Circled alone in the stainless sky.

So the dove flew to the Rajah's tower —
  Fled from the slaughter of Moslem kings;
So the thorns covered the city of Gaur,
  And Dacca was lost for a white dove's wings.
Dove — dove — oh, homing dove,
  Dacca is lost from the roll of the kings!

THE EXPLANATION

Love and Death once ceased their strife
At the Tavern of Man's Life.
Called for wine, and threw — alas!—
Each his quiver on the grass.
When the bout was o'er they found
Mingled arrows strewed the ground.
Hastily they gathered then
Each the loves and lives of men.
Ah, the fateful dawn deceived!
Mingled arrows each one sheaved;
Death's dread armoury was stored
With the shafts he most abhorred;
Love's light quiver groaned beneath
Venom-headed darts of Death.

Thus it was they wrought our woe
At the Tavern long ago.
Tell me, do our masters know,
Loosing blindly as they fly,
Old men love while young men die?

AN ANSWER

A ROSE, in tatters on the garden path,
Cried out to God and murmured 'gainst His wrath,
Because a sudden wind at twilight's hush
Had snapped her stem alone of all the bush.
And God, who hears both sun-dried dust and sun,
Made answer whispering to that luckless one,
"Sister, in that thou sayest We did not well —
"What voices heardst thou when thy petals fell?"
And the Rose answered, "In that evil hour
"A voice said, 'Father, wherefore falls the flower?
" 'For lo, the very gossamers are still.'
"And a voice answered, 'Son, by Allah's will!' "
Then softly as a rain-mist on the sward,
Came to the Rose the Answer of the Lord:
"Sister, before We smote the dark in twain,
"Ere yet the stars saw one another plain,
"Time, tide, and space, We bound unto the task
"That thou shouldst fall, and such an one should
    ask."

Whereat the withered flower, all content,
Died as they die whose days are innocent;
While he who questioned why the flower fell
Caught hold of God and saved his soul from Hell.

THE GIFT OF THE SEA

THE dead child lay in the shroud,
   And the widow watched beside;
And her mother slept, and the Channel swept
   The gale in the teeth of the tide.

But the mother laughed at all.
   "I have lost my man in the sea,
"And the child is dead. Be still," she said,
   "What more can ye do to me?"

The widow watched the dead,
   And the candle guttered low,
And she tried to sing the Passing Song
   That bids the poor soul go.

And "Mary take you now," she sang,
   "That lay against my heart."
And "Mary smooth your crib to-night,"
   But she could not say "Depart."

Then came a cry from the sea,
   But the sea-rime blinded the glass,
      And "Heard ye nothing, mother?" she said,
   "'Tis the child that waits to pass."

And the nodding mother sighed.
   "'Tis a lambing ewe in the whin,
"For why should the christened soul cry out,
   "That never knew of sin?"

"O feet I have held in my hand,
   "O hands at my heart to catch,
"How should they know the road to go,
   "And how should they lift the latch?"

They laid a sheet to the door,
   With the little quilt atop,
That it might not hurt from the cold or the dirt,
   But the crying would not stop.

The widow lifted the latch
   And strained her eyes to see,
And opened the door on the bitter shore
   To let the soul go free.

There was neither glimmer nor ghost,
　There was neither spirit nor spark,
And "Heard ye nothing, mother?" she said,
　"'Tis crying for me in the dark."

And the nodding mother sighed,
　"'Tis sorrow makes ye dull;
"Have ye yet to learn the cry of the tern,
　"Or the wail of the wind-blown gull?"

"The terns are blown inland,
　"The grey gull follows the plough.
"'Twas never a bird, the voice I heard,
　"O mother, I hear it now!"

"Lie still, dear lamb, lie still;
　"The child is passed from harm,
"'Tis the ache in your breast that broke your rest
　"And the feel of an empty arm."

She put her mother aside,
　"In Mary's name let be!
"For the peace of my soul I must go," she said,
　And she went to the calling sea.

In the heel of the wind-bit pier,
  Where the twisted weed was piled,
She came to the life she had missed by an hour,
  For she came to a little child.

She laid it into her breast,
  And back to her mother she came,
But it would not feed and it would not heed.
  Though she gave it her own child's name.

And the dead child dripped on her breast,
  And her own in the shroud lay stark;
And "God forgive us, mother," she said
  "We let it die in the dark!"

EVARRA AND HIS GODS

Read here,
This is the story of Evarra — man —
Maker of Gods in lands beyond the sea.

Because the city gave him of her gold,
Because the caravans brought turquoises,
Because his life was sheltered by the King,
So that no man should maim him, none should
    steal,
Or break his rest with babble in the streets
When he was weary after toil, he made
An image of his God in gold and pearl,
With turquoise diadem and human eyes,
A wonder in the sunshine, known afar
And worshipped by the King; but, drunk with
    pride,
Because the city bowed to him for God,
He wrote above the shrine: *"Thus Gods are made,*
"And whoso makes them otherwise shall die."
And all the city praised him. . . . Then he died.

Read here the story of Evarra — man —
Maker of Gods in lands beyond the sea.

  Because the city had no wealth to give,
  Because the caravans were spoiled afar,
  Because his life was threatened by the King,
  So that all men despised him in the streets,
  He hewed the living rock, with sweat and tears,
  And reared a God against the morning-gold,
  A terror in the sunshine, seen afar,
  And worshipped by the King; but, drunk with
      pride,
  Because the city fawned to bring him back,
  He carved upon the plinth: "*Thus Gods are made,*
  "*And whoso makes them otherwise shall die.*"
  And all the people praised him. . . . Then he
      died.

Read here the story of Evarra — man —
Maker of Gods in lands beyond the sea.

  Because he lived among a simple folk,
  Because his village was between the hills,
  Because he smeared his cheeks with blood of ewes,
  He cut an idol from a fallen pine,
  Smeared blood upon its cheeks, and wedged a shell

Above its brows for eyes, and gave it hair
Of trailing moss, and plaited straw for crown.
And all the village praised him for this craft,
And brought him butter, honey, milk, and curds.
Wherefore, because the shoutings drove him mad,
He scratched upon that log: "*Thus Gods are made,*
"*And whoso makes them otherwise shall die.*"
And all the people praised him. . . . Then he
      died.

Read here the story of Evarra — man —
Maker of Gods in lands beyond the sea.
Because his God decreed one clot of blood
Should swerve one hair's-breadth from the pulse's
      path,
And chafe his brain, Evarra mowed alone,
Rag-wrapped, among the cattle in the fields,
Counting his fingers, jesting with the trees,
And mocking at the mist, until his God
Drove him to labour.   Out of dung and horns
Dropped in the mire he made a monstrous God,
Abhorrent, shapeless, crowned with plaintain tufts,
And when the cattle lowed at twilight time,
He dreamed it was the clamour of lost crowds,

And howled among the beasts: "*Thus Gods are
     made,*
"*And whoso makes them otherwise shall die.*"
Thereat the cattle bellowed. . . . Then he died.

Yet at the last he came to Paradise,
And found his own four Gods, and that he wrote;
And marvelled, being very near to God,
What oaf on earth had made his toil God's law,
Till God said mocking: "Mock not. These be
     thine."
Then cried Evarra: "I have sinned!"—"Not so.
"If thou hadst written otherwise, thy Gods
"Had rested in the mountain and the mine,
"And I were poorer by four wondrous Gods,
"And thy more wondrous law, Evarra. Thine,
"Servant of shouting crowds and lowing kine."

Thereat, with laughing mouth, but tear-wet eyes,
Evarra cast his Gods from Paradise.

*This is the story of Evarra — man —
Maker of Gods in lands beyond the sea.*

THE CONUNDRUM OF THE WORKSHOPS

WHEN the flush of a new-born sun fell first on
    Eden's green and gold,
Our father Adam sat under the Tree and scratched
    with a stick in the mould;
And the first rude sketch that the world had seen
    was joy to his mighty heart,
Till the Devil whispered behind the leaves, ''It's
    pretty, but is it Art?''

Wherefore he called to his wife, and fled to fashion
    his work anew —
The first of his race who cared a fig for the first,
    most dread review;
And he left his lore to the use of his sons — and
    that was a glorious gain
When the Devil chuckled ''Is it Art?'' in the ear
    of the branded Cain.

They builded a tower to shiver the sky and wrench
    the stars apart,
Till the Devil grunted behind the bricks: "It's
    striking, but is it Art?"
The stone was dropped at the quarry-side and the
    idle derrick swung,
While each man talked of the aims of Art, and
    each in an alien tongue.

They fought and they talked in the North and
    the South, they talked and they fought in
    the West,
Till the waters rose on the pitiful land, and the
    poor Red Clay had rest —
Had rest till the dank, blank-canvas dawn when the
    dove was preened to start,
And the Devil bubbled below the keel: "It's
    human, but is it Art?"

The tale is as old as the Eden Tree — and new as
    the new-cut tooth —
For each man knows ere his lip-thatch grows he is
    master of Art and Truth;

And each man hears as the twilight nears, to the
    beat of his dying heart,
The Devil drum on the darkened pane: "You did
    it, but was it Art?"

We have learned to whittle the Eden Tree to the
    shape of a surplice-peg,
We have learned to bottle our parents twain in the
    yelk of an addled egg,
We know that the tail must wag the dog, for the
    horse is drawn by the cart;
But the Devil whoops, as he whooped of old "It's
    clever, but is it Art?"

When the flicker of London sun falls faint on the
    Club-room's green and gold,
The sons of Adam sit them down and scratch with
    their pens in the mould —
They scratch with their pens in the mould of their
    graves, and the ink and the anguish start,
For the Devil mutters behind the leaves: "It's
    pretty, but is it Art?"

Now, if we could win to the Eden Tree where the
    Four Great Rivers flow,
And the Wreath of Eve is red on the turf as she
    left it long ago,
And if we could come when the sentry slept and
    softly scurry through,
By the favour of God we might know as much —
    as our father Adam knew.

IN THE NEOLITHIC AGE

In the Neolithic Age savage warfare did I wage
    For food and fame and two-toed horses' pelt;
I was singer to my clan in that dim, red Dawn of
    Man,
    And I sang of all we fought and feared and felt.

Yea, I sang as now I sing, when the Prehistoric spring
    Made the piled Biscayan ice-pack split and shove,
And the troll and gnome and dwerg, and the Gods
    of Cliff and Berg
    Were about me and beneath me and above.

But a rival of Solutré told the tribe my style was
    outré —
    By a hammer, grooved of dolomite, he fell.
And I left my views on Art, barbed and tanged,
    beneath the heart
    Of a mammothistic etcher at Grenelle.

Then I stripped them, scalp from skull, and my hunt-
    ing dogs fed full,
    And their teeth I threaded neatly on a thong;

And I wiped my mouth and said, "It is well that
    they are dead,
  "For I know my work is right and theirs was
    wrong."

But my Totem saw the shame; from his ridgepole
    shrine he came,
  And he told me in a vision of the night:—
"There are nine and sixty ways of constructing
    tribal lays,
  "And every single one of them is right!"

.   .   .   .

Then the silence closed upon me till They put new
    clothing on me
  Of whiter, weaker flesh and bone more frail;
And I stepped beneath Time's finger once again a
    tribal singer
  And a minor poet certified by Tr—l.

Still they skirmish to and fro, men my messmates on
    the snow,
  When we headed off the aurochs turn for turn;
When the rich Allobrogenses never kept amanuenses,
  And our only plots were piled in lakes at Berne.

Still a cultured Christian age sees us scuffle, squeak,
and rage,
  Still we pinch and slap and jabber — scratch and
  dirk;
Still we let our business slide — as we dropped the
half-dressed hide —
  To show a fellow-savage how to work.

Still the world is wondrous large,— seven seas from
marge to marge,—
  And it holds a vast of various kinds of man;
And the wildest dreams of Kew are the facts of
Khatmandhu
  And the crimes of Clapham chaste in Martaban.

Here's my wisdom for your use, as I learned it when
the moose
  And the reindeer roared where Paris roars to-night:
There are nine and sixty ways of constructing
tribal lays,
  And—every—single—one—of—them—is—right.

THE LEGEND OF EVIL

I

THIS is the sorrowful story
  Told when the twilight fails
And the monkeys walk together
  Holding each other's tails.

"Our fathers lived in the forest,
  "Foolish people were they,
"They went down to the cornland
  "To teach the farmers to play.

"Our fathers frisked in the millet,
  "Our fathers skipped in the wheat,
"Our fathers hung from the branches,
  "Our fathers danced in the street.

"Then came the terrible farmers,
  "Nothing of play they knew,
"Only . . . they caught our fathers
  "And set them to labour too!

"Set them to work in the cornland
  "With ploughs and sickles and flails,
"Put them in mud-walled prisons
  "And — cut off their beautiful tails!

"Now, we can watch our fathers,
  "Sullen and bowed and old,
"Stooping over the millet,
  "Sharing the silly mould.

"Driving a foolish furrow,
  "Mending a muddy yoke,
"Sleeping in mud-walled prisons,
  "Steeping their food in smoke.

"We may not speak to our fathers,
  "For if the farmers knew
"They would come up to the forest
  "And set us to labour too!"

This is the horrible story
  Told as the twilight fails
And the monkeys walk together
  Holding each other's tails.

II

'TWAS when the rain fell steady an' the Ark was
    pitched an' ready,
  That Noah got his orders for to take the bastes
    below;
He dragged them all together by the horn an' hide
    an' feather,
  An' all excipt the Donkey was agreeable to go.

Thin Noah spoke him fairly, thin talked to him
    sevarely,
  An' thin he cursed him squarely to the glory
    av the Lord:
"Divil take the ass that bred you, and the greater
    ass that fed you —
  Divil go wid you, ye spalpeen!" an' the Donkey
    went aboard.

But the wind was always failin', an' 'twas most
    onaisy sailin',
  An' the ladies in the cabin couldn't stand the
    stable air;

An' the bastes betwuxt the hatches, they tuk an'
    died in batches,
  Till Noah said: "There's wan av us that hasn't
    paid his fare!"

For he heard a flusteration wid the bastes av all
    creation —
  The trumpetin' av elephints an' bellowin' av
    whales;
An' he saw forninst the windy whin he wint to
    stop the shindy
  The Divil wid a stable-fork bedivillin' their tails.

The Divil cursed outrageous, but Noah said um-
    brageous:
  "To what am I indebted for this tenant-right
    invasion?"
An' the Divil gave for answer: "Evict me if you
    can, sir,
  "For I came in wid the Donkey — on Your
    Honour's invitation."

THE ENGLISH FLAG

*Above the portico a flag-staff, bearing the Union
Jack, remained flutering in the flames for some time,
but ultimately when it fell the crowds rent the air with
shouts, and seemed to see significance in the incident.*
— Daily Papers.

WINDS of the World, give answer? They are
    whimpering to and fro —
And what should they know of England who only
    England know?—
The poor little street-bred people that vapour and
    fume and brag,
They are lifting their heads in the stillness to yelp
    at the English Flag!

Must we borrow a clout from the Boer — to plaster
    anew with dirt?
An Irish liar's bandage, or an English coward's
    shirt?
We may not speak of England; her Flag's to sell or
    share.
What is the Flag of England? Winds of the
    World, declare!

The North Wind blew:—"From Bergen my steel-
shod-van-guards go;

"I chase your lazy whalers home from the Disko
floe;

"By the great North Lights above me I work the
will of God,

"That the liner splits on the ice-field or the Dogger
fills with cod.

"I barred my gates with iron, I shuttered my doors
with flame,

"Because to force my ramparts your nutshell navies
came;

"I took the sun from their presence, I cut them
down with my blast,

"And they died, but the Flag of England blew free
ere the spirit passed.

"The lean white bear hath seen it in the long, long
Arctic night,

"The musk-ox knows the standard that flouts the
Northern Light:

"What is the Flag of England? Ye have but my
bergs to dare,

"Ye have but my drifts to conquer. Go forth, for
it is there!"

The South Wind sighed:—"From The Virgins my
  mid-sea course was ta'en
"Over a thousand islands lost in an idle main,
"Where the sea-egg flames on the coral and the
  long-backed breakers croon
"Their endless ocean legends to the lazy, locked
  lagoon.

"Strayed amid lonely islets, mazed amid outer
  keys,
"I waked the palms to laughter — I tossed the scud
  in the breeze —
"Never was isle so little, never was sea so lone,
"But over the scud and the palm-trees an English
  flag was flown.

"I have wrenched it free from the halliard to hang
  for a wisp on the Horn;
"I have chased it north to the Lizard — ribboned
  and rolled and torn;
"I have spread its fold o'er the dying, adrift in a
  hopeless sea;
"I have hurled it swift on the slaver, and seen the
  slave set free.

"My basking sunfish know it, and wheeling albatross,
"Where the lone wave fills with fire beneath the
    Southern Cross.
"What is the Flag of England? Ye have but my
    reefs to dare,
"Ye have but my seas to furrow.   Go forth, for it is
    there!"

The East Wind roared:—"From the Kuriles, the
    Bitter Seas, I come,
"And me men call the Home-Wind, for I bring the
    English home.
"Look — look well to your shipping!   By the breath
    of my mad typhoon
"I swept your close-packed Praya and beached your
    best at Kowloon!

"The reeling junks behind me and the racing seas
    before,
"I raped your richest roadstead — I plundered Singa-
    pore!
"I set my hand on the Hoogli; as a hooded snake
    she rose,
"And I flung your stoutest steamers to roost with
    the startled crows.

"Never the lotos closes, never the wild-fowl wake,

"But a soul goes out on the East Wind that died for
England's sake —

"Man or woman or suckling, mother or bride or
maid —

"Because on the bones of the English the English
Flag is stayed.

"The desert-dust hath dimmed it, the flying wild-ass
knows

"The scared white leopard winds it across the taint-
less snows.

"What is the Flag of England?   Ye have but my
sun to dare,

"Ye have but my sands to travel.   Go forth, for it is
there!"

The West Wind called:—"In squadrons the thought-
less galleons fly

"That bear the wheat and cattle lest street-bred
people die.

"They make my might their porter, they make my
house their path,

"Till I loose my neck from their rudder and whelm
them all in my wrath.

"I draw the gliding fog-bank as a snake is drawn
from the hole;

"They bellow one to the other, the frighted ship-
bells toll,

"For day is a drifting terror till I raise the shroud
with my breath,

"And they see strange bows above them and the
two go locked to death.

"But whether in calm or wrack-wreath, whether by
dark or day,

"I heave them whole to the conger or rip their
plates away,

"First of the scattered legions, under a shrieking sky,

"Dipping between the rollers, the English Flag goes
by.

"The dead dumb fog hath wrapped it — the frozen
dews have kissed —

"The naked stars have seen it, a fellow-star in the
mist.

"What is the Flag of England? Ye have but my
breath to dare,

"Ye have but my waves to conquer. Go forth, for
it is there!"

"CLEARED"

(IN MEMORY OF A COMMISSION)

HELP for a patriot distressed, a spotless spirit
hurt,
Help for an honourable clan sore trampled in the
dirt!
From Queenstown Bay to Donegal, O listen to my
song,
The honourable gentlemen have suffered grievous
wrong.

Their noble names were mentioned — O the burning
black disgrace!—
By a brutal Saxon paper in an Irish shooting-
case;
They sat upon it for a year, then steeled their heart
to brave it,
And "coruscating innocence" the learned Judges
gave it.

117

Bear witness, Heaven, of that grim crime beneath
the surgeon's knife,
The honourable gentleman deplored the loss of
life;
Bear witness of those chanting choirs that burk and
shirk and snigger,
No man laid hand upon the knife or finger to the
trigger!

Cleared in the face of all mankind beneath the
winking skies,
Like phœnixes from Phœnix Park (and what lay
there) they rise!
Go shout it to the emerald seas — give word to Erin
now,
Her honourable gentlemen are cleared — and this
is how:—

They only paid the Moonlighter his cattle-hocking
price,
They only helped the murderer with council's best
advice,

But — sure it keeps their honour white — the
    learned Court believes
They never gave a piece of plate to murderers and
    thieves.

They never told the ramping crowd to card a
    woman's hide,
They never marked a man for death — what fault of
    theirs he died?—
They only said "intimidate," and talked and went
    away —
By God, the boys that did the work were braver
    men than they!

Their sin it was that fed the fire — small blame to
    them that heard —
The "bhoys" get drunk on rhetoric, and madden
    at the word —
They knew whom they were talking at, if they
    were Irish too,
The gentlemen that lied in Court, they knew and
    well they knew.

They only took the Judas-gold from Fenians out of
  jail,
They only fawned for dollars on the blood-eyed
  Clan-na-Gael.
If black is black or white is white, in black and
  white it's down,
They're only traitors to the Queen and rebels to
  the Crown.

"Cleared," honourable gentlemen.   Be thankful it's
  no more:—
The widow's curse is on your house, the dead are
  at your door.
On you the shame of open shame, on you from
  North to South
The hand of every honest man flat-heeled across
  your mouth.

"Less black than we were painted"?— Faith, no
  word of black was said;
The lightest touch was human blood, and that, ye
  know, runs red.

It's sticking to your fist to-day for all your sneer
    and scoff,
And by the Judge's well-weighed word you cannot
    wipe it off.

Hold up those hands of innocence — go, scare your
    sheep together,
The blundering, tripping tups that bleat behind the
    old bell-wether;
And if they snuff the taint and break to find another
    pen,
Tell them it's tar that glistens so, and daub them
    yours again!

"The charge is old"?— As old as Cain — as fresh as
    yesterday;
Old as the Ten Commandments, have ye talked
    those laws away?
If words are words, or death is death, or powder
    sends the ball,
You spoke the words that sped the shot — the curse
    be on you all.

"Our friends believe"? Of course they do — as
    sheltered women may;
But have they seen the shrieking soul ripped from
    the quivering clay?
They!— If their own front door is shut, they'll
    swear the whole world's warm;
What do they know of dread of death or hanging
    fear of harm?

The secret half a county keeps, the whisper in the
    lane,
The shriek that tells the shot went home behind
    the broken pane,
The dry blood crisping in the sun that scares the
    honest bees,
And shows the "bhoys" have heard your talk —
    what do they know of these?

But you — you know — ay, ten times more; the
    secrets of the dead,
Black terror on the country-side by word and
    whisper bred.

The mangled stallion's scream at night, the tail-
    cropped heifer's low.
Who set the whisper going first? You know, and
    well you know!

My soul! I'd sooner lie in jail for murder plain
    and straight,
Pure crime I'd done with my own hand for money,
    lust, or hate,
Than take a seat in Parliament by fellow-felons
    cheered,
While one of those "not provens" proved me cleared
    as you are cleared.

Cleared — you that "lost" the league accounts —
    go, guard our honour still,
Go, help to make our country's laws that broke
    God's law at will —
One hand stuck out behind the back, to signal
    "strike again";
The other on your dress-shirt-front to show your
    heart is clane.

If black is black or white is white, in black and
    white it's down,
You're only traitors to the Queen and rebels to the
    Crown.
If print is print or words are words, the learned
    Court perpends:
We are not ruled by murderers, but only — by their
    friends.

AN IMPERIAL RESCRIPT

Now this is the tale of the Council the German
    Kaiser decreed,
To ease the strong of their burden, to help the
    weak in their need
He sent a word to the peoples, who struggle, and
    pant, and sweat,
That the straw might be counted fairly and the
    tally of bricks be set.

The Lords of Their Hands assembled; from the
    East and the West they drew —
Baltimore, Lille, and Essen, Brummagem, Clyde,
    and Crewe.
And some were black from the furnace, and some
    were brown from the soil,
And some were blue from the dye-vat; but all were
    wearied of toil.

And the young King said, "I have found it, the
    road to the rest ye seek;
"The strong shall wait for the weary, the hale shall
    halt for the weak;
"With the even tramp of an army where no man
    breaks from the line,
"Ye shall march to peace and plenty in the bond of
    brotherhood — sign!"

The paper lay on the table, the strong heads bowed
    thereby,
And a wail went up from the peoples: "Ay, sign —
    give rest, for we die!"
A hand was stretched to the goose-quill, a fist was
    cramped to scrawl,
When — the laugh of a blue-eyed maiden ran clear
    through the council-hall.

And each one heard Her laughing as each one saw
    Her plain —
Saidie, Mimi, or Olga, Gretchen, or Mary Jane.
And the Spirit of Man that is in Him to the light
    of the vision woke;
And the men drew back from the paper, as a
    Yankee delegate spoke:—

"There's a girl in Jersey City who works on the
    telephone;
"We're going to hitch our horses and dig for a
    house of our own,
"With gas and water connections, and steam-heat
    through to the top;
"And, W. Hohenzollern, I guess I shall work till
    I drop."

And an English delegate thundered: "The weak
    an' the lame be blowed!
"I've a berth in the Sou'-West workshops, a home
    in the Wandsworth Road;
"And till the 'sociation has footed my buryin' bill,
"I work for the kids an' the missis. Pull up! I'll
    be damned if I will!"

And over the German benches the bearded whisper
    ran:—
"Lager, der girls und der dollars, dey makes or dey
    breaks a man.
"If Schmitt haf collared der dollars, he collars der
    girl deremit;
"But if Schmitt bust in der pizness, we collars der
    girl from Schmitt."

They passed one resolution: "Your sub-committee
believe

"You can lighten the curse of Adam when you've
lightened the curse of Eve.

"But till we are built like angels — with hammer
and chisel and pen,

"We will work for ourself and a woman, for ever
and ever.   Amen."

Now this is the tale of the Council the German
Kaiser held —

The day that they razored the Grindstone, the
day that the Cat was belled,

The day of the Figs from Thistles, the day of the
Twisted Sands,

The day that the laugh of a maiden made light of
the Lords of Their Hands.

TOMLINSON

Now Tomlinson gave up the ghost in his house in
    Berkeley Square,
And a Spirit came to his bedside and gripped him
    by the hair —
A Spirit gripped him by the hair and carried him
    far away,
Till he heard as the roar of rain-fed ford the roar
    of the Milky Way,
Till he heard the roar of the Milky Way die down
    and drone and cease,
And they came to the Gate within the Wall where
    Peter holds the keys.

"Stand up, stand up now, Tomlinson, and answer
    loud and high
"The good that ye did for the sake of men or ever
    ye came to die —
"The good that ye did for the sake of men in little
    earth so lone!"'

And the naked soul of Tomlinson grew white as
 a rain-washed bone.

"O, I have a friend on earth," he said, "that was
 my priest and guide,

"And well would he answer all for me if he were by
 my side."

—"For that ye strove in neighbour-love it shall be
 written fair,

"But now ye wait at Heaven's Gate and not in
 Berkeley Square:

"Though we called your friend from his bed this
 night, he could not speak for you,

"For the race is run by one and one and never by
 two and two."

Then Tomlinson looked up and down, and little
 gain was there,

For the naked stars grinned overhead, and he saw
 that his soul was bare:

The Wind that blows between the worlds, it cut
 him like a knife,

And Tomlinson took up his tale and spoke of his
 good in life.

"This I have read in a book," he said, "and that
 was told to me,

"And this I have thought that another man thought
   of a Prince in Muscovy."

The good souls flocked like homing doves and
   bade him clear the path,

And Peter twirled the jangling keys in weariness
   and wrath.

"Ye have read, ye have heard, ye have thought," he
   said, "and the tale is yet to run:

"By the worth of the body that once ye had, give
   answer — what ha' ye done?"

Then Tomlinson looked back and forth, and little
   good it bore,

For the Darkness stayed at his shoulder-blade and
   Heaven's Gate before:

"Oh, this I have felt, and this I have guessed, and
   this I have heard men say,

"And this they wrote that another man wrote of a
   carl in Norroway."

"Ye have read, ye have felt, ye have gussed, good
   lack! Ye have hampered Heaven's Gate;

"There's little room between the stars in idleness to
   prate!

"Oh, none may reach by hired speech of neighbour
   priest, and kin,

"Through borrowed deed to God's good meed that
　　lies so fair within;

"Get hence, get hence to the Lord of Wrong, for
　　doom has yet to run,

"And . . . the faith that ye share with Berkeley
　　Square uphold you, Tomlinson!"

　　.　　.　　.　　.　　.　　.　　.　　.　　.　　.

The Spirit gripped him by the hair, and sun by sun
　　they fell

Till they came to the belt of Naughty Stars that
　　rim the mouth of Hell:

The first are red with pride and wrath, the next are
　　white with pain,

But the third are black with clinkered sin that
　　cannot burn again:

They may hold their path, they may leave their
　　path, with never a soul to mark,

They may burn or freeze, but they must not cease
　　in the Scorn of the Outer Dark.

The Wind that blows between the worlds, it nipped
　　him to the bone,

And he yearned to the flare of Hell-gate there as
　　the light of his own hearth-stone.

The Devil he sat behind the bars, where the desperate legions drew,

But he caught the hasting Tomlinson and would not let him through.

"Wot ye the price of good pit-coal that I must pay?" said he,

"That ye rank yoursel' so fit for Hell and ask no leave of me?

"I am all o'er-sib to Adam's breed that ye should give me scorn,

"For I strove with God for your First Father the day that he was born.

"Sit down, sit down upon the slag, and answer loud and high

"The harm that ye did to the Sons of Men or ever you came to die."

And Tomlinson looked up and up, and saw against the night

The belly of a tortured star blood-red in Hell-Mouth light;

And Tomlinson looked down and down, and saw beneath his feet

The frontlet of a tortured star milk-white in Hell-Mouth heat.

"Oh, I had a love on earth," said he, "that kissed
 me to my fall,

"And if ye would call my love to me I know she
 would answer all."

—"All that ye did in love forbid it shall be written
 fair,

"But now ye wait at Hell-Mouth Gate and not in
 Berkeley Square:

"Though we whistled your love from her bed to-
 night I trow she would not run,

"For the sin ye do by two and two ye must pay for
 one by one!"

The Wind that blows between the worlds, it cut
 him like a knife,

And Tomlinson took up the tale and spoke of his
 sin in life:

"Once I ha' laughed at the power of Love and twice
 at the grip of the Grave,

"And thrice I ha' patted my God on the head that
 men might call me brave."

The Devil he blew on a brandered soul and set it
 aside to cool:

"Do ye think I would waste my good pit-coal on the
 hide of a brain-sick fool?

"I see no worth in the hobnailed mirth or the jolt-
head jest ye did

"That I should waken my gentlemen that are sleeping three on a grid."

Then Tomlinson looked back and forth, and there
was little grace,

For Hell-Gate filled the houseless Soul with the
Fear of Naked Space.

"Nay, this I ha' heard," quo' Tomlinson, "and this
was noised abroad,

"And this I ha' got from a Belgian book on the word
of a dead French lord."

—"Ye ha' heard, ye ha' read, ye ha' got, good lack!
And the tale begins afresh —

"Have ye sinned one sin for the pride o' the eye or
the sinful lust of the flesh?"

Then Tomlinson he gripped the bars and yammered
"Let me in —

"For I mind that I borrowed my neighbour's wife to
sin the deadly sin."

The Devil he grinned behind the bars, and banked
the fires high:

"Did ye read of that sin in a book?" said he; and
Tomlinson said "Ay!"

The Devil he blew upon his nails, and the little
  devils ran;
And he said, "Go husk this whimpering thief that
  comes in the guise of a man:
"Winnow him out 'twixt star and star, and sieve his
  proper worth:
"There's sore decline in Adam's line if this be
  spawn of earth."
Empusa's crew, so naked-new they may not face the
  fire,
But weep that they bin too small to sin to the height
  of their desire,
Over the coal they chased the Soul, and racked it
  all abroad,
As children rifle a caddis-case or the raven's foolish
  hoard,
And back they came with the tattered Thing, as
  children after play,
And they said: "The soul that he got from God he
  has bartered clean away.
"We have threshed a stook of print and book, and
  winnowed a chattering wind
"And many a soul wherefrom he stole, but his we
  cannot find:

"We have handled him, we have dandled him, we
    have seared him to the bone,

"And sure if tooth and nail show truth he has no soul
    of his own."

The Devil he bowed his head on his breast and
    rumbled deep and low:—

"I'm all o'er-sib to Adam's breed that I should bid
    him go.

"Yet close we lie, and deep we lie, and if I gave him
    place,

"My gentlemen that are so proud would flout me to
    my face;

"They'd call my house a common stews and me a
    careless host,

"And — I would not anger my gentlemen for the sake
    of a shiftless ghost."

The Devil he looked at the mangled Soul that
    prayed to feel the flame.

And he thought of Holy Charity, but he thought of
    his own good name:

"Now ye could haste my coal to waste, and sit ye
    down to fry:

"Did ye think of that theft for yourself?" said he;
    and Tomlinson said "Ay!"

The Devil he blew an outward breath, for his heart
    was free from care:

"Ye have scarce the soul of a louse," he said, "but
    the roots of sin are there,

"And for that sin should ye come in were I the lord
    alone.

"But sinful pride has rule inside — and mightier than
    my own.

"Honour and Wit, fore-damned they sit, to each his
    priest and whore:

"Nay, scarce I dare myself go there, and you they'd
    torture sore.

"Ye are neither spirit nor spirk," he said; "ye are
    neither book nor brute —

"Go, get ye back to the flesh again for the sake of
    Man's repute.

"I'm all o'er-sib to Adam's breed that I should mock
    your pain,

"But look that ye win to worthier sin ere ye come
    back again.

"Get hence, the hearse is at your door — the grim
    black stallions wait —

"They bear your clay to place to-day.   Speed, lest
    ye come too late!

"Go back to Earth with a lip unsealed — go back
    with an open eye,

"And carry my word to the Sons of Men or ever ye
    come to die:

"That the sin they do by two and two they must pay
    for one by one —

"And . . . the God that you took from a printed
    book be with you, Tomlinson!"

BARRACK-ROOM BALLADS

To **T. A.**

I have made for you a song,
And it may be right or wrong,
But only you can tell me if it's true;
I have tried for to explain
Both your pleasure and your pain,
And, Thomas, here's my best respects to you!
Oh, there'll surely come a day
When they'll grant you all your pay,
And treat you as a Christian ought to do;
So, until that day comes round,
Heaven keep you safe and sound,
And, Thomas, here's my best respects to you.

R. K.

DANNY DEEVER

"WHAT are the bugles blowin' for?" said Files-on-
Parade.

"To turn you out, to turn you out," the Colour-
Sergeant said.

"What makes you look so white, so white?" said
Files-on-Parade.

"I'm dreadin' what I've got to watch," the Colour-
Sergeant said.

For they're hangin' Danny Deever, you can
hear the Dead March play,

The regiment's in 'ollow square — they're
hangin' him to-day;

They've taken of his buttons off an' cut his
stripes away,

An' they're hangin' Danny Deever in the
mornin.'

"What makes the rear-rank breathe so 'ard?" said
  Files-on-Parade.
"It's bitter cold, it's bitter cold," the Colour-
  Sergeant said.
"What makes that front-rank man fall down?" says
  Files-on-Parade.
"A touch o' sun, a touch o' sun," the Colour-
  Sergeant said.

> They are hangin' Danny Deever, they are
>   marchin' of 'im round,
> They 'ave 'alted Danny Deever by 'is coffin
>   on the ground;
> An' 'e'll swing in 'arf a minute for a sneakin'
>   shootin' hound —
> O they're hangin' Danny Deever in the
>   mornin'!

"'Is cot was right-'and cot to mine," said Files-on-
  Parade.
"E's sleepin' out an' far to-night," the Colour-
  Sergeant said.
"I've drunk 'is beer a score o' times," said Files-on-
  Parade.
"E's drinkin' bitter beer alone," the Colour-Sergeant
  said.

They are hangin' Danny **Deever**, you must
  mark 'im to 'is place,
For 'e shot a comrade sleepin'— you must
  look 'im in the face;
Nine 'undred of 'is county an' the regiment's
  disgrace,
While they're hangin' Danny Deever in the
  mornin'.

"What's that so black agin the sun?" said Files-on-
  Parade.
"It's Danny fightin' 'ard for life," the Colour-
  Sergeant said.
"What's that that whimpers over'ead?" said Files-
  on-Parade.
"It's Danny's soul that's passin' now," the Colour-
  Sergeant said.

For they're done with Danny Deever, you
  can 'ear the quickstep play,
The regiment's in column, an' they're
  marchin' us away;
Ho! the young recruits are shakin', an'
  they'll want their beer to-day,
After hangin' Danny Deever in the
  mornin'.

TOMMY

I WENT into a public-'ouse to get a pint o' beer,
The publican 'e up an' sez, "We serve no red-coats
here."
The girls be'ind the bar they laughed an' giggled
fit to die,
I outs into the street again an' to myself sez I:

O it's Tommy this, an' Tommy that, an'
"Tommy, go away";
But it's "Thank you, Mister Atkins," when
the band begins to play,
The band begins to play, my boys, the band
begins to play,
O it's "Thank you, Mister Atkins," when the
band begins to play.

I went into a theatre as sober as could be,
They gave a drunk civilian room, but 'adn't none
for me;

They sent me to the gallery or round the music-'alls,
But when it comes to fightin', Lord! they'll shove
   me in the stalls!

      For it's Tommy this, an' Tommy that, an'
         "Tommy, wait outside";
      But it's "Special train for Atkins" when the
         trooper's on the tide,
      The troopship's on the tide, my boys, the
         troopship's on the tide,
      O it's "Special train for Atkins" when the
         trooper's on the tide.

Yes, makin' mock o' uniforms that guard you while
   you sleep
Is cheaper than them uniforms, an' they're starva-
   tion cheap;
An' hustlin' drunken soldiers when they're goin'
   large a bit
Is five times better business than paradin' in full kit.

      Then it's Tommy this, an' Tommy that,
         an' "Tommy, 'ow's yer soul?"
      But it's 'Thin red line of 'eroes' when the
         drums begin to roll,

> The drums begin to roll, my boys, the drums
>   begin to roll,
>   O it's "Thin red line of 'eroes" when the
>   drums begin to roll.

We aren't no thin red 'eroes, nor we aren't no black-
    guards too,
But single men in barricks, most remarkable like
    you;
An' if sometimes our conduck isn't all your fancy
    paints:
Why, single men in barricks don't grow into plaster
    saints;

> While it's Tommy this, an' Tommy that, an'
>   "Tommy, fall be'ind,"
> But it's "Please to walk in front, sir," when
>   there's trouble in the wind,
> There's trouble in the wind, my boys, there's
>   trouble in the wind,
>   O it's "Please to walk in front, sir," when
>   there's trouble in the wind.

You talk o' better food for us, an' schools, an' fires,
    an' all:
We'll wait for extry rations if you treat us rational,

Don't mess about the cook-room slops, but prove it
    to our face
The Widow's Uniform is not the soldier-man's dis-
    grace.

      For it's Tommy this, an' Tommy that, an'
         "Chuck him out, the brute!"
      But it's "Saviour of 'is country," when the
         guns begin to shoot;
      Yes it's Tommy this, an' Tommy that, an'
         anything you please;
      But Tommy ain't a bloomin' fool — you bet
         that Tommy sees!

"FUZZY-WUZZY"

SOUDAN EXPEDITIONARY FORCE

We've fought with many men acrost the seas,
  An' some of 'em was brave an' some was not
The Paythan an' the Zulu an' Burmese;
  But the Fuzzy was the finest o' the lot.
We never got a ha'porth's change of 'im:
  'E squatted in the scrub an' 'ocked our 'orses.
'E cut our sentries up at Sua*kim*,
    An' 'e played the cat an' banjo with our forces.

> So 'ere's *to* you, Fuzzy-Wuzzy, at your 'ome
>   in the Soudan;
> You're a pore benighted 'eathen but a first-
>   class fightin' man;
> We gives you your certificate, an' if you want
>   it signed
> We'll come an' 'ave a romp with you when-
>   ever you're inclined.

150

We took our chanst among the Kyber 'ills,
    The Boers knocked us silly at a mile,
The Burman give us Irriwaddy chills,
    An' a Zulu *impi* dished us up in style:
But all we ever got from such as they
    Was pop to what the Fuzzy made us swaller;
We 'eld our bloomin' own, the papers say,
    But man for man the Fuzzy knocked us 'oller.
        Then 'ere's *to* you, Fuzzy-Wuzzy, an' the
            missis and the kid;
        Our orders was to break you, an' of course
            we went an' did.
        We sloshed you with Martinis, an' it wasn't
            'ardly fair;
        But for all the odds agin' you, Fuzzy-Wuzzy
            you broke the square.

'E 'asn't got no papers of 'is own,
    'E 'asn't got no medals nor rewards,
So we must certify the skill 'e's shown
    In usin' of 'is long two-'anded swords:
When 'e's 'oppin' in an' out among the bush
    With 'is coffin-'eaded shield an' shovel-spear,
An 'appy day with Fuzzy on the rush
    Will last an 'ealthy Tommy for a year.

So 'ere's *to* you, Fuzzy-Wuzzy, an' your
friends which are no more,
If we 'adn't lost some messmates we would
'elp you to deplore;
But give an' take's the gospel, an' we'll call
the bargain fair,
For if you 'ave lost more than us, you
crumpled up the square!

'E rushes at the smoke when we let drive,
An', before we know, 'e's 'ackin' at our 'ead;
'E's all 'ot sand an' ginger when alive,
An' 'e's generally shammin' when 'e's dead.
'E's a daisy, 'e's a ducky, 'e's a lamb!
'E's a injia-rubber idiot on the spree,
'E's the on'y thing that doesn't give a damn
For a Regiment o' British Infantree!
So 'ere's *to* you, Fuzzy-Wuzzy, at your 'ome
in the Soudan;
You're a pore benighted 'eathen but a first-
class fightin' man;
An' 'ere's *to* you, Fuzzy-Wuzzy, with your
'ayrick 'ead of 'air —
You big black boundin' beggar — for you
broke a British square!

SOLDIER, SOLDIER

"Soldier, soldier, come from the wars,
Why don't you march with my true love?"
"We're fresh from off the ship an' 'e's maybe give
    the slip,
An' you'd best go look for a new love."

    New love!   True love!
    Best go look for a new love,
    The dead they cannot rise, an' you'd better
        dry your eyes,
    An' you'd best go look for a new love.

"Soldier, soldier, come from the wars,
What did you see o' my true love?"
"I seed ' im serve the Queen in a suit o' rifle-green,
An' you'd best go look for a new love."

"Soldier, soldier, come from the wars,
Did ye see no more o' my true love?"

"I seed 'im runnin' by when the shots begun to fly —
But you'd best go look for a new love."

"Soldier, soldier, come from the wars,
Did aught take 'arm to my true love?"
"I couldn't see the fight, for the smoke it lay so
      white —
An' you'd best go look for a new love."

"Soldier, soldier, come from the wars,
I'll up an' tend to my true love!"
"'E's lying on the dead with a bullet through 'is 'ead,
An' you'd best go look for a new love."

"Soldier, soldier, come from the wars,
I'll down an' die with my true love!"
"The pit we dug'll 'ide 'im an' the twenty men beside
      'im —
An' you'd best go look for a new love."

"Soldier, soldier, come from the wars,
Do you bring no sign from my true love?"
"I bring a lock of 'air that 'e allus used to wear,
An' you'd best go look for a new love."

"Soldier, soldier, come from the wars,
O then I know it's true I've lost my true love!"
"An' I tell you truth again — when you've lost the
      feel o' pain
You'd best take me for your true love."

> True love!   New love!
> Best take 'im for a new love.
> The dead they cannot rise, an' you'd better
>   dry your eyes,
> An' you'd best take 'im for your true love.

SCREW-GUNS

SMOKIN' my pipe on the mountings, sniffin' the
    mornin' cool,
I walks in my old brown gaiters along o' my old
    brown mule,
With seventy gunners be'ind me, an' never a beggar
    forgets
It's only the pick of the Army that handles the
    dear little pets — 'Tss! 'Tss!

    For you all love the screw-guns, the screw-
        guns they all love you!
    So when we call round with a few guns, o'
        course you will know what to do — hoo!
        hoo!
    Jest send in your Chief an' surrender — it's
        worse if you fights or you runs:
    You can go where you please, you can skid
        up the trees, but you don't get away
        from the guns.

They sends us along where the roads are, but mostly
    we goes where they ain't:
We'd climb up the side of a sign-board an' trust to
    the stick o' the paint:
We've chivied the Naga an' Looshai, we've give the
    Afreedeeman fits,
For we fancies ourselves at two thousand, we guns
    that are built in two bits — 'Tss! 'Tss!
      For you all love the screw-guns, etc.

If a man doesn't work, why, we drills 'im an' teaches
    'im 'ow to behave;
If a beggar can't march, why, we kills 'im an' rattles
    'im into 'is grave.
You've got to stand up to our business an' spring
    without snatchin' or fuss.
D'you say that you sweat with the field guns? By
    God, you must lather with us —'Tss! 'Tss!
      For you all love the screw-guns, etc.

The eagles is screamin' around us, the river's a-
    moanin' below,
We're clear o' the pine an' the oak-scrub, we're out
    on the rocks an' the snow,

An' the wind is as thin as a whip-lash what carries
    away to the plains
The rattle an' stamp o' the lead-mules — the
    jinglety-jink o' the chains — 'Tss! 'Tss!
      For you all love the screw-guns, etc.

There's a wheel on the Horns o' the Mornin', an' a
    wheel on the edge o' the Pit,
An' a drop into nothin' beneath you as straight as a
    beggar can spit:
With the sweat runnin' out o' your shirt-sleeves, an'
    the sun off the snow in your face,
An' 'arf o' the men on the drag-ropes to hold the
    old gun in 'er place — 'Tss! 'Tss!
      For you all love the screw-guns, etc.

Smokin' my pipe on the mountings, sniffin' the
    mornin' cool,
I climbs in my old brown gaiters along o' my old
    brown mule.
The monkey can say what our road was — the wild-
    goat 'e knows where we passed.
Stand easy, you long-eared old darlin's! Out drag-
    ropes! With shrapnel! Hold fast — 'Tss! 'Tss!

For you all love the screw-guns — the screw-
    guns they all love you!
So when we take tea with a few guns, o'
    course you will know what to do — hoo!
    hoo!
Just send in your Chief and surrender — it's
    worse if you fights or you runs:
You may hide in the caves, they'll be only
    your graves, but you can't get away from
    the guns!

CELLS

I'VE a head like a concertina: I've a tongue like a
    button-stick:
I've a mouth like an old potato, and I'm more than
    a little sick,
But I've had my fun o' the Corp'rals Guard: I've
    made the cinders fly,
And I'm here in the Clink for a thundering drink
    and blacking the Corporal's eye.

    With a second-hand overcoat under my head,
      And a beautiful view of the yard,
Oh, it's pack-drill for me and a fortnight's **C.B.**
      For "drunk and resisting the Guard!"
      Mad drunk and resisting the Guard —
        'Strewth, but I socked it them hard!
So it's pack-drill for me and a fortnight's **C.B.**
      For "drunk and resisting the Guard."

I started o' canteen porter, I finished o' canteen
    beer,
But a dose o' gin that a mate slipped in, it was that
    brought me here.
'Twas that and an extry double Guard that rubbed
    my nose in the dirt;
But I fell away with the Corp'ral's stock and the
    best of the Corp'ral's shirt.

I left my cap in a public-house, my boots in the
    public road,
And Lord knows where, and I don't care, my belt
    and my tunic goed,
They'll stop my pay, they'll cut away the stripes I
    used to wear,
But I left my mark on the Corp'ral's face, and I
    think he'll keep it there!

My wife she cries on the barrack-gate, my kid in
    the barrack-yard,
It ain't that I mind the Ord'ly room — it's *that* that
    cuts so hard.

I'll take my oath before them both that I will sure
    abstain,
But as soon as I'm in with a mate and gin, I know
    I'll do it again!

    With a second-hand overcoat under my head
    And a beautiful view of the yard,
Yes, it's pack-drill for me and a fortnight's C.B.
    For "drunk and resisting the Guard."
      Mad drunk and resisting the Guard —
      'Strewth, but I socked it them hard!—
So it's pack-drill with me and a fortnight's C.B.
    For "drunk and resisting the Guard."

GUNGA DIN

You may talk o' gin and beer
When you're quartered safe out 'ere,
An' you're sent to penny-fights an' Aldershot it;
But when it comes to slaughter
You will do your work on water,
An' you'll lick the bloomin' boots of 'im that's got it.
Now in Injia's sunny clime,
Where I used to spend my time
A-servin' of 'Er Majesty the Queen,
Of all them black-faced crew
The finest man I knew
Was our regimental bhisti, Gunga Din.
 He was "Din! Din! Din!
 You limping lump o' brick-dust, Gunga Din!
 Hi! slippery hitherao!
 Water, get it! Panee lao![1]
 You squigy-nosed old idol, Gunga Din."

The uniform 'e wore
Was nothin' much before,

[1] Bring water swiftly.

163

An' rather less than 'arf o' that be'ind,
For a piece o' twisty rag
An' a goatskin water-bag
Was all the field-equipment 'e could find.
When the sweatin' troop-train lay
In a sidin' through the day,
Where the 'eat would make your bloomin' eyebrows
    crawl,
We shouted "Harry By!"[1]
Till our throats were bricky-dry,
Then we wopped 'im 'cause 'e couldn't serve us all.
    It was "Din! Din! Din!
    You 'eathen, where the mischief 'ave you
        been?
    You put some juldee[2] in it
    Or I'll marrow[3] you this minute
    If you don't fill up my helmet, Gunga Din!

    'E would dot an' carry one
    Till the longest day was done
An' 'e didn't seem to know the use o' fear.
    If we charged or broke or cut,
    You could bet your bloomin' nut,
"E'd be waitin' fifty paces right flank rear.

[1]Mr. Atkins' equivalent for "O brother."
[2]Be quick.   [3]Hit you.

With 'is mussick[1] on 'is back,
'E would skip with our attack,
An' watch us till the bugles made "Retire,"
An' for all 'is dirty 'ide
'E was white, clear white, inside
When 'e went to tend the wounded under fire!
It was "Din! Din! Din!"
With the bullets kickin' dust-spots on the green
When the cartridges ran out,
You could hear the front-files shout,
"Hi! ammunition-mules an' Gunga Din!"

I sha'n't forgit the night
When I dropped be'ind the fight
With a bullet where my belt plate should 'a' been.
I was chokin' mad with thirst,
An' the man that spied me first
Was our good old grinnin', gruntin' Gunga Din.
'E lifted up my 'ead,
An' he plugged me where I bled,
An' 'e guv me 'arf-a-pint o' water-green:
It was crawlin' and it stunk,
But of all the drinks I've drunk,
I'm gratefullest to one from Gunga Din.

[1] Water skins.

It was 'Din! Din! Din!"
'Ere's a beggar with a bullet through 'is spleen;
　　'E's chawin' up the ground,
　　An' 'e's kickin' all around:
For Gawd's sake git the water, Gunga Din!

　　'E carried me away
　　To where a dooli lay,
An' a bullet come an' drilled the beggar clean.
　　'E put me safe inside,
　　An' just before 'e died:
"I 'ope you liked your drink," sez Gunga Din.
　　So I'll meet 'im later on
　　At the place where 'e is gone —
Where it's always double drill and no canteen;
　　'E'll be squattin' on the coals,
　　Givin' drink to poor damned souls,
An' I'll get a swig in hell from Gunga Din!
　　Yes, Din! Din! Din!
　You Lazarushian-leather Gunga Din!
　　　Though I've belted you and flayed you,
　　　By the living Gawd that made you,
　　You're a better man than I am, Gunga Din!

OONTS

(NORTHERN INDIA TRANSPORT TRAIN)

Wot makes the soldier's 'eart to penk, wot makes
    him to perspire?
It isn't standin' up to charge nor lyin' down to fire;
But it's everlastin' waitin' on a everlastin' road
For the commissariat camel an' 'is commissariat load.
      O the oont,[1] O the oont, O the commissariat
        oont!
        With 'is silly neck a-bobbin' like a basket
          full o' snakes;
        We packs 'im like an idol, an' you ought to
          'ear 'im grunt,
          An' when we gets 'im loaded up 'is blessed
            girth-rope breaks.

Wot makes the rear-guard swear so 'ard when night
    is drorin' in,
An' every native follower is shiverin' for 'is skin?

[1] Camel — *oo* is pronounced like *u* in " bull," but by Mr. Atkins to rhyme
with " front."

167

It ain't the chanst o' being rushed by Paythans from
the 'ills,
It's the commissariat camel puttin' on 'is bloomin'
frills!
O the oont, O the oont, O the hairy, scary
oont!
A-trippin' over tent-ropes when we've got
the night alarm!
We socks 'im with a stretcher-pole an' 'eads
'im off in front,
An' when we've saved 'is bloomin' life 'e
chaws our bloomin' arm.

The 'orse 'e knows above a bit, the bullock's but a
fool,
The elephant's a gentleman, the battery-mule's a
mule;
But the commissariat cam-u-el, when all is said an'
done,
'E's a devil an' a ostrich an' a orphan-child in one.
O the oont, O the oont, O the Gawd-forsaken
oont!
The lumpy-'umpy 'ummin'-bird a-singin'
where 'e lies,

'E's blocked the whole division from the
rear-guard to the front,
 An' when we get him up again — the
beggar goes an' dies!

'E'll gall an' chafe an' lame an' fight — 'e smells
most awful vile;
'E'll lose 'isself for ever if you let 'im stray a mile;
'E's game to graze the 'ole day long an' 'owl the
'ole night through,
An' when 'e comes to greasy ground 'e splits 'isself
in two.
 O the oont, O the oont, O the floppin',
droppin' oont!
 When 'is long legs give from under an' 'is
meltin' eye is dim,
 The tribes is up be'ind us, and the tribes
is out in front —
 It ain't no jam for Tommy, but it's kites
an' crows for 'im.

So when the cruel march is done, an' when the
roads is blind,
An' when we sees the camp in front an' 'ears the
shots be'ind,

Ho then we strips 'is saddle off, and all 'is woes is
    past:
'E thinks on us that used 'im so, and gets revenge
    at last.
        O the oont, O the oont, O the floatin',
            bloatin' oont!
        The late lamented camel in the water-cut
            'e lies;
    We keeps a mile behind 'im an' we keeps a
        mile in front,
        But 'e gets into the drinkin'-casks, and
            then o' course we dies.

LOOT

IF you've ever stole a pheasant-egg be'ind the
 keeper's back,
 If you've ever snigged the washin' from the line,
If you've ever crammed a gander in your bloomin'
 'aversack,
 You will understand this little song o' mine.
But the service rules are 'ard, and from such we
 are debarred,
 For the same with English morals does not suit.
 (*Cornet:* Toot! toot!)
W'y, they call a man a robber if 'e stuffs 'is marchin'
 clobber
With the —
(*Chorus.*) Loo! loo! Lulu! lulu! Loo! loo! Loot!
 loot! loot!
 Ow the loot!
 Bloomin' loot!
 That's the thing to make the boys git up an'
 shoot!

171

It's the same with dogs an' men,
If you'd make 'em come again
Clap 'em forward with a Loo! loo! Lulu!
Loot!
(*ff*) Whoopee! Tear 'im, puppy! Loo! loo! Lulu!
Loot! loot! loot!

If you've knocked a nigger edgeways when 'e's
thrustin' for your life,
You must leave 'im very careful where 'e fell;
An' may thank your stars an' gaiters if you didn't
feel 'is knife
That you ain't told off to bury 'im as well.
Then the sweatin' Tommies wonder as they spade
the beggars under
Why lootin' should be entered as a crime;
So if my song you'll 'ear, I will learn you plain an'
clear
'Ow to pay yourself for fightin' overtime
(*Chorus.*)   With the loot, etc.

Now remember when you're 'acking round a gilded
Burma god
That 'is eyes is very often precious stones;

An' if you treat a nigger to a dose o' cleanin'-rod
   'E's like to show you everything 'e owns.
When 'e won't prodooce no more, pour some water
    on the floor
   Where you 'ear it answer 'ollow to the boot
      (*Cornet:* Toot! toot!)—
When the ground begins to sink, shove your baynick
    down the chink,
   An' you're sure to touch the —
(*Chorus.*)   Loo! loo! Lulu! Loot! loot! loot!
           Ow the loot! etc.

When from 'ouse to 'ouse you're 'unting, you must
    always work in pairs —
   It 'alves the gain, but safer you will find —
For a single man gets bottled on them twisty-wisty
    stairs,
   An' a woman comes and clobs 'im from be'ind.
When you've turned 'em inside out, an' it seems
    beyond a doubt
   As if there weren't enough to dust a flute
      (*Cornet:* Toot! toot!)—

Before you sling your 'ook, at the 'ouse-tops take a
    look,
  For it's underneath the tiles they 'ide the loot.
    (*Chorus.*) Ow the loot, etc.

You can mostly square a Sergint an' a Quartermaster
    too,
  If you only take the proper way to go;
I could never keep my pickin's, but I've learned
    you all I knew —
  An' don't you never say I told you so.
An' now I'll bid good-by, for I'm gettin' rather dry,
  An' I see another tunin' up to toot (*Cornet:* Toot!
    toot) —!
So 'ere's good-luck to those that wears the Widow's
    clo'es,
  An' the Devil send 'em all they want o' loot!
    (*Chorus.*) Yes, the loot,
           Bloomin' loot.
  In the tunic an' the mess-tin an' the boot!
    It's the same with dogs an' men,
    If you'd make 'em come again
(*fff*) Whoop 'em forward with a Loo! loo! Lulu!
    Loot! loot! loot!
Heeya! Sick 'im, puppy! Loo! loo! Lulu! Loot!
    loot! loot!

"SNARLEYOW"

This 'appened in a battle to a batt'ry of the corps
Which is first among the women an' amazin' first
    in war;
An' what the bloomin' battle was I don't remember
    now,
But Two's off-lead 'e answered to the name o'
    Snarleyowl.

    Down in the Infantry, nobody cares;
    Down in the Cavalry, Colonel 'e swears;
    But down in the lead with the wheel at the flog
    Turns the bold Bombardier to a little whipped
        dog!

They was movin' into action, they was needed very
    sore,
To learn a little schoolin' to a native army corps,

They 'ad nipped against an uphill, they was tuckin'
    down the brow,
When a tricky, trundlin' round-shot give the knock
    to *Snarleyow*.

They cut 'im loose an' left 'im — 'e was almost tore
    in two —
But he tried to follow after as a well-trained 'orse
    should do;
'E went an' fouled the limber, an' the Driver's
    Brother squeals:
"Pull up, pull up for *Snarleyow* — 'is 'ead's between
    'is 'eels!"

The Driver 'umped 'is shoulder, for the wheels was
    goin' round,
An' there aren't no "Stop, conductor!" when a
    batt'ry's changin' ground;
Sez 'e: "I broke the beggar in, an' very sad I feels,
But I couldn't pull up, not for *you* — your 'ead
    between your 'eels!"

'E 'adn't 'ardly spoke the word, before a droppin'
    shell
A little right the batt'ry an' between the sections fell;

An' when the smoke 'ad cleared away, before the
  limber wheels,
There lay the Driver's Brother with 'is 'ead between
  'is 'eels.

Then sez the Driver's Brother, an' 'is words was very
  plain,
"For Gawd's own sake get over me, an' put me out
  o' pain."
They saw 'is wounds was mortial, an' they judged
  that it was best,
So they took an' drove the limber straight across 'is
  back an' chest.

The Driver 'e give nothin' 'cept a little coughin'
  grunt,
But 'e swung 'is 'orses 'andsome when it came to
  "Action front!"
An' if one wheel was juicy, you may lay your Mon-
  day head
'Twas juicier for the niggers when the case begun
  to spread.

The moril of this story, it is plainly to be seen:
You 'avn't got no families when servin' of the Queen—

You 'avn't got no brothers, fathers, sisters, wives, or
    sons —
If you want to win your battles take an' work your
    bloomin' guns!

    Down in the Infantry, nobody cares;
    Down in the Cavalry, Colonel 'e swears;
    But down in the lead with the wheel at the
        flog
    Turns the bold Bombardier to a little
        whipped dog!

THE WIDOW AT WINDSOR

'AVE you 'eard o' the Widow at Windsor
   With a hairy gold crown on 'er 'ead?
She 'as ships on the foam — she 'as millions at 'ome,
   An' she pays us poor beggars in red.
     (Ow, poor beggars in red!)
There's 'er nick on the cavalry 'orses,
   There's 'er mark on the medical stores —
An' 'er troopers you'll find with a fair wind be'ind
   That takes us to various wars.
     (Poor beggars!— barbarious wars!)

    Then 'ere's to the Widow at Windsor,
      An' 'ere's to the stores an' the guns,
    The men an' the 'orses what makes up the
      forces
      O' Missis Victorier's sons.
       (Poor beggars!   Victorier's sons!)

Walk wide o' the Widow at Windsor,
  For 'alf o' Creation she owns:
We 'ave bought 'er the same with the sword an'
      the flame,
  An' we've salted it down with our bones.
      (Poor beggars! — it's blue with our bones!)
Hands off o' the sons of the Widow,
  Hands off o' the goods in 'er shop,
For the Kings must come down an' the Emperors
      frown
  When the Widow at Windsor says "Stop"!
      (Poor beggars! — we're sent to say "Stop"!)

      Then 'ere's to the Lodge o' the Widow,
        From the Pole to the Tropics it runs —
      To the Lodge that we tile with the rank
          an' the file,
        An' open in form with the guns.
          (Poor beggars! — it's always the guns!)

We 'ave 'eard o' the Widow at Windsor,
  It's safest to leave 'er alone:
For 'er sentries we stand by the sea an' the land
  Wherever the bugles are blown.
      (Poor beggars! — an' don't we get blown!)

Take 'old o' the Wings o' the Mornin',
　An' flop round the earth till you're dead;
But you won't get away from the tune that they play
　To the bloomin' old Rag over'ead.
　　(Poor beggars! — it's 'ot over'ead!)

　　Then 'ere's to the sons o' the Widow
　　　Wherever, 'owever they roam.
　　'Ere's all they desire, an' if they require
　　　A speedy return to their 'ome.
　　　　(Poor　　beggars!— they'll　never　see
　　　　　'ome!)

BELTS

THERE was a row in Silver Street that's near to
    Dublin Quay,
Between an Irish regiment an' English cavalree;
It started at Revelly an' it lasted on till dark:
The first man dropped at Harrison's, the last forninst
    the Park.

    For it was "Belts, belts, belts, an' that's one
        for you!"
    An' it was "Belts, belts, belts, an' that's done
        for you!"
    O buckle an' tongue
    Was the song that we sung
    From Harrison's down to the Park!

There was a row in Silver Street — the regiments
    was out,
They called us "Delhi Rebels," an' we answered
    "Threes about!"

That drew them like a hornet's nest — we met them
    good an' large,
The English at the double an' the Irish at the
    charge.
        Then it was : Belts —

There was a row in Silver Street — an' I was in it
    too;
We passed the time o' day, an' then the belts went
    whirraru!
I misremember what occurred, but subsequint the
    storm
A *Freeman's Journal Supplemint* was all my uniform.
        O it was: Belts —

There was a row in Silver Street — they sent the
    Polis there,
The English were too drunk to know, the Irish
    didn't care;
But when they grew impertinint we simultaneous
    rose,
Till half o' them was Liffey mud an' half was
    tatthered clo'es.
        For it was: Belts —

There was a row in Silver Street — it might ha'
    raged till now,
But some one drew his side-arm clear, an' nobody
    knew how;
'Twas Hogan took the point an' dropped; we saw
    the red blood run:
An' so we all was murderers that started out in fun.
        While it was: Belts —

There was a row in Silver Street — but that put
    down the shine,
Wid each man whisperin' to his next: " 'Twas never
    work o' mine!"
We went away like beaten dogs, an' down the street
    we bore him,
The poor dumb corpse that couldn't tell the bhoys
    were sorry for him.
        When it was: Belts —

There was a row in Silver Street — it isn't over
    yet,
For half of us are under guard wid punishments to
    get;

'Tis all a merricle to me as in the Clink I lie:
There was a row in Silver Street — begod, I wonder
    why!
      But it was "Belts, belts, belts, an' that's one
        for you!"
      An' it was "Belts, belts, belts, an' that's done
        for you!"
      O buckle and tongue
      Was the song that we sung
      From Harrison's down to the Park!

THE YOUNG BRITISH SOLDIER

WHEN the 'arf-made recruity goes out to the East
'E acts like a babe an' 'e drinks like a beast,
An' 'e wonders because 'e is frequent deceased
  Ere 'e's fit for to serve as a soldier,
   Serve, serve, serve as a soldier,
   Serve, serve, serve as a soldier,
   Serve, serve, serve as a soldier,
    So-oldier *of* the Queen!

Now all you recruities what's drafted to-day,
You shut up your rag-box an' 'ark to my lay,
An' I'll sing you a soldier as far as I may:
  A soldier what's fit for a soldier.
   Fit, fit, fit for a soldier.

First mind you steer clear o' the grog-sellers' huts,
For they sell you Fixed Bay'nets that rots out your
  guts —
Ay, drink that 'ud eat the live steel from your butts—
  An' it's bad for the young British soldier.
   Bad, bad, bad for the soldier.

When the cholera comes — as it will past a doubt —
Keep out of the wet and don't go on the shout,
For the sickness gets in as the liquor dies out,
      An' it crumples the young British soldier.
           Crum-, crum-, crumples the soldier. . .

But the worst o' your foes is the sun over'ead:
You *must* wear your 'elmet for all that is said:
If 'e finds you uncovered 'e'll knock you down
    dead,
      An' you'll die like a fool of a soldier.
        Fool, fool, fool of a soldier. . .

If you're cast for fatigue by a sergeant unkind,
Don't grouse like a woman nor crack on nor
    blind;
Be handy and civil and then you will find
      That it's beer for the young British soldier.
        Beer, beer, beer for the soldier.

Now, if you must marry, take care she is old —
A troop-sergeant's widow's the nicest I'm told —
For beauty won't help if your rations is cold,
      Nor love ain't enough for a soldier,
        'Nough, 'nough, 'nough for a soldier. . .

If the wife should go wrong with a comrade, be loth
To shoot when you catch 'em — you'll swing, on my
     oath!--
Make 'im take 'er and keep 'er: that's Hell for
     them both,
          An' you're shut o' the curse of a soldier.
               Curse, curse, curse o' a soldier. . .

When first under fire an' you're wishful to duck,
Don't look nor take 'eed at the man that is struck,
Be thankful you're livin', and trust to your luck
          And march to your front like a soldier.
               Front, front, front like a soldier. . .

When 'arf of your bullets fly wide in the ditch,
Don't call your Martini a cross-eyed old bitch;
She's human as you are — you treat her as sich,
          An' she'll fight for the young British soldier.
               Fight, fight, fight for the soldier. . .

When shakin' their bustles like ladies so fine,
The guns o' the enemy wheel into line;
Shoot low at the limbers an' don't mind the shine,
          For noise never startles the soldier.
               Start-, start-, startles the soldier. . .

If your officer's dead and the sergeants look white,
Remember it's ruin to run from a fight:
So take open order, lie down, and sit tight,
    And wait for supports like a soldier.
       Wait, wait, wait like a soldier. . .

When you're wounded and left on Afghanistan's
    plains,
And the women come out to cut up what remains,
Jest roll to your rifle and blow out your brains
    An' go to your Gawd like a soldier.
      Go, go, go like a soldier,
      Go, go, go like a soldier,
      Go, go, go like a soldier,
       So-oldier *of* the Queen!

MANDALAY

By the old Moulmein Pagoda, lookin' eastward to
    the sea,
There's a Burma girl a-settin', and I know she
    thinks o' me;
For the wind is in the palm-trees, and the temple-
    bells they say:
"Come you back, you British soldier; come you back
    to Mandalay!"

    Come you back to Mandalay,
    Where the old Flotilla lay;
    Can't you 'ear their paddles chunkin' from
        Rangoon to Mandalay,
    On the road to Mandalay,
    Where the flyin'-fishes play,
    An' the dawn comes up like thunder outer
        China 'crost the Bay!

'Er petticoat was yaller an' 'er little cap was green,
An' 'er name was Supi-yaw-lat — jes' the same as
    Theebaw's Queen,

190

An' I seed her first a-smokin' of a whackin' white
cheroot,
An' a-wastin' Christian kisses on an 'eathen idol's
foot:

> Bloomin' idol made o' mud —
> What they called the Great Gawd Budd —
> Plucky lot she cared for idols when I kissed
> 'er where she stud!
> On the road to Mandalay, etc.

When the mist was on the rice-fields an' the sun
was droppin' slow,
She'd git her little banjo an' she'd sing "*Kulla-
lo-lo!*"
With 'er arm upon my shoulder an' 'er cheek agin
my cheek
We useter watch the steamers an' the *hathis* pilin'
teak.

> Elephints a-pilin' teak
> In the sludgy, squdgy creek,
> Where the silence 'ung that 'eavy you was
> 'arf afraid to speak!
> On the road to Mandalay, etc.

But that's all shove be'ind me — long ago an' fur
  away,
An' there ain't no 'busses runnin' from the Bank to
  Mandalay;
An' I'm learnin' 'ere in London what the ten-year
  soldier tells:
"If you've 'eard the East a-callin', you won't never
  'eed naught else."

> No! you won't 'eed nothin' else
> But them spicy garlic smells,
> An' the sunshine an' the palm-trees an' the
>   tinkly temple-bells;
> On the road to Mandalay, etc.

I am sick o' wastin' leather on these gritty pavin'
  stones,
An' the blasted Henglish drizzle wakes the fever in
  my bones;
Tho' I walks with fifty 'ousemaids outer Chelsea to
  the Strand,
An' they talks a lot o' lovin', but wot do they
  understand?

> Beefy face an' grubby 'and —
> Law! wot do they understand?

I've a neater, sweeter maiden in a cleaner,
  greener land!
On the road to Mandalay, etc.

Ship me somewheres east of Suez, where the best is
  like the worst,
Where there aren't no Ten Commandments an' a
  man can raise a thirst;
For the temple-bells are callin', and it's there that
  I would be —
By the old Moulmein Pagoda, looking lazy at the
  sea:

  On the road to Mandalay,
  Where the old Flotilla lay,
  With our sick beneath the awnings when we
    went to Mandalay!
  Oh the road to Mandalay,
  Where the flyin'-fishes play,
  An' the dawn comes up like thunder outer
    China 'crost the Bay!

TROOPIN'

(OUR ARMY IN THE EAST)

TROOPIN', troopin', troopin' to the sea:
'Ere's September come again — the six-year men
    are free.
O leave the dead be'ind us, for they cannot come
    away
To where the ship's a-coalin' up that takes us 'ome
    to-day.

> We're goin' 'ome, we're goin' 'ome,
> Our ship is *at* the shore,
> An' you must pack your 'aversack,
> For we won't come back no more.
> Ho, don't you grieve for me,
> My lovely Mary-Ann,
> For I'll marry you yit on a fourp'ny bit
> As a time-expired man!

The Malabar's in 'arbour with the Jumner at 'er tail,
An' the time-expired's waitin' of 'is orders for to
    sail.
Ho! the weary waitin' when on Khyber 'ills we lay,
But the time-expired's waitin' of 'is orders 'ome
    to-day.

They'll turn us out at Portsmouth wharf in cold an'
    wet an' rain,
All wearin' Injian cotton kit, but we will not com-
    plain;
They'll kill us of pneumonia — for that's their little
    way —
But damn the chills and fever, men, we're goin'
    'ome to-day!

Troopin', troopin', winter's round again!
See the new draf's pourin' in for the old campaign;
Ho, you poor recruities, but you've got to earn your
    pay —
What's the last from Lunnon, lads? We're goin'
    there to-day.

Troopin', troopin,' give another cheer —
'Ere's to English women an' a quart of English beer;

The Colonel an' the regiment an' all who've got to
 stay,
Gawd's mercy strike 'em gentle — Whoop! we're
 goin' 'ome to-day.

  We're goin' 'ome, we're goin' 'ome,
  Our ship is at the shore,
  An' you must pack your 'aversack,
  For we won't come back no more.
  Ho, don't you grieve for me,
  My lovely Mary-Ann,
  For I'll marry you yit on a fourp'ny bit
  As a time-expired man.

THE WIDOW'S PARTY

"WHERE have you been this while away,
        Johnnie, Johnnie?"
Out with the rest on a picnic lay,
        Johnnie, my Johnnie, aha!
They called us out of the barrack-yard
To Gawd knows where from Gosport Hard,
And you can't refuse when you get the card,
        And the Widow gives the party.
        (*Bugle.*)   Ta—rara—ra-ra-rara!

"What did you get to eat and drink,
        Johnnie, Johnnie?"
Standing water as thick as ink,
        Johnnie, my Johnnie, aha!
A bit o' beef that were three year stored,
A bit o' mutton as tough as a board,
And a fowl we killed with a sergeant's sword,
        When the Widow give the party.

"What did you do for knives and forks,
                    Johnnie, Johnnie?"
We carries 'em with us wherever we walks,
                    Johnnie, my Johnnie, aha!
And some was sliced and some was halved,
And some was crimped and some was carved,
And some was gutted and some was starved,
                    When the Widow give the party.

"What ha' you done with half your mess,
                    Johnnie, Johnnie?"
They couldn't do more and they wouldn't do less
                    Johnnie, my Johnnie, aha!
They ate their whack and they drank their fill,
And I think the rations has made them ill,
For half my comp'ny's lying still
                    Where the Widow give the party.

"How did you get away — away,
                    Johnnie, Johnnie?"
On the broad o' my back at the end o' the day,
                    Johnnie, my Johnnie, aha!

I comed away like a bleedin' toff,
For I got four niggers to carry me off,
As I lay in the bight of a canvas trough,
       When the Widow give the party.

"What was the end of all the show,
       Johnnie, Johnnie?"
Ask my Colonel, for I don't know,
       Johnnie, my Johnnie, aha!
We broke a King and we built a road —
A court-house stands where the reg'ment goed.
And the river's clean where the raw blood flowed
       When the widow give the party.
         (*Bugle.*) Ta—rara—ra-ra-rara!

FORD O' KABUL RIVER

Kabul town's by Kabul river —
  Blow the bugle, draw the sword —
There I lef' my mate for ever,
  Wet an' drippin' by the ford.
    Ford, ford, ford o' Kabul river,
      Ford o' Kabul river in the dark!
    There's the river up and brimmin', an' there's
      'arf a squadron swimmin'
      'Cross the ford o' Kabul river in the dark.

Kabul town's a blasted place —
  Blow the bugle, draw the sword —
'Strewth I shan't forget 'is face
  Wet an' drippin' by the ford!
    Ford, ford, ford o' Kabul river,
      Ford o' Kabul river in the dark!
    Keep the crossing-stakes beside you, an' they
      will surely guide you
      'Cross the ford of Kabul river in the dark.

Kabul town is sun and dust —
  Blow the bugle, draw the sword —
I'd ha' sooner drownded fust
  'Stead of 'im beside the ford.
    Ford, ford, ford o' Kabul river,
      Ford o' Kabul river in the dark!
    You can 'ear the 'orses threshin', you can
        'ear the men a-splashin',
      'Cross the ford o' Kabul river in the dark.

Kabul town was ours to take —
  Blow the bugle, draw the sword —
I'd ha' left it for 'is sake —
  'Im that left me by the ford.
    Ford, ford, ford o' Kabul river,
      Ford o' Kabul river in the dark!
    It's none so bloomin' dry there; ain't you
        never comin' nigh there,
      'Cross the ford o' Kabul river in the dark?

Kabul town'll go to hell —
  Blow the bugle, draw the sword —
'Fore I see him 'live an' well —
  'Im the best beside the ford.

Ford, ford, ford o' Kabul river,
Ford o' Kabul river in the dark!
Gawd 'elp 'em if they blunder, for their
boots'll pull 'em under,
By the ford o' Kabul river in the dark.

Turn your 'orse from Kabul town —
Blow the bugle, draw the sword —
'Im an' 'arf my troop is down,
Down an' drownded by the ford.
Ford, ford, ford o' Kabul river,
Ford o' Kabul river in the dark!
There's the river low an' fallin', but it ain't
no use o' callin'
'Cross the ford o' Kabul river in the dark.

GENTLEMEN-RANKERS

To the legion of the lost ones, to the cohort of the
    damned,
  To my brethren in their sorrow overseas,
Sings a gentleman of England cleanly bred, ma-
    chinely crammed,
  And a trooper of the Empress, if you please.
Yea, a trooper of the forces who has run his own six
    horses,
  And faith he went the pace and went it blind,
And the world was more than kin while he held the
    ready tin,
  But to-day the Sergeant's something less than kind.
      We're poor little lambs who've lost our way,
        Baa! Baa! Baa!
      We're little black sheep who've gone astray,
        Baa — aa — aa!
      Gentlemen-rankers out on the spree
      Damned from here to Eternity,
      God ha' mercy on such as we,
        Baa! Yah! Bah!

Copyright, 1892, by Macmillan & Co.

Oh, it's sweet to sweat through stables, sweet to
     empty kitchen slops,
   And it's sweet to hear the tales the troopers tell,
To dance with blowzy housemaids at the regimental
     hops,
   And thrash the cad who says you waltz too well.
Yes, it makes you cock-a-hoop to be "Rider" to
     your troop,
   And branded with a blasted worsted spur,
When you envy, Oh, how keenly, one poor Tommy
     being cleanly
   Who blacks your boots and sometimes call you
     "Sir."

If the home we never write to, and the oaths we
     never keep,
   And all we know most distant and most dear,
Across the snoring barrack-room return to break our
     sleep,
   Can you blame us if we soak ourselves in beer?
When the drunken comrade mutters and the great
     guard-lantern gutters
   And the horror of our fall is written plain,
Every secret, self-revealing on the aching white-
     washed ceiling,
   Do you wonder that we drug ourselves from pain?

We have done with Hope and Honour, we are lost
    to Love and Truth,
  We are dropping down the ladder rung by rung,
And the measure of our torment is the measure of
    our youth.
  God help us, for we knew the worst too young!
Our shame is clean repentance for the crime that
    brought the sentence,
  Our pride it is to know no spur of pride,
And the Curse of Reuben holds us till an alien turf
    enfolds us
  And we die, and none can tell Them where we
    died.
      We're poor little lambs who've lost our way,
        Baa! Baa! Baa!
      We're little black sheep who've gone astray,
        Baa — aa — aa!
      Gentlemen-rankers out on the spree,
      Damned from here to Eternity,
      God ha' mercy on such as we,
        Baa! Yah! Bah!

ROUTE MARCHIN'

WE'RE marchin' on relief over Injia's sunny plains,
A little front o' Christmas time an' just be'ind the
    Rains,
Ho! get away, you bullock-man, you've 'eard the
    bugle blowed,
There's a regiment a-comin' down the Grand Trunk
    Road;
    With its best foot first
    And the road a-sliding past,
    An' every bloomin' campin'-ground exactly
        like the last;
    While the Big Drum says,
    With 'is "*rowdy-dowdy-dow!*" —
    "*Kiko kissy warsti* don't you *hamsher argyjow?*"

Oh, there's them Injian temples to admire when you
    see,
There's the peacock round the corner an' the
    monkey up the tree,

An' there's that rummy silver grass a-wavin' in the
  wind,

An' the old Grand Trunk a trailin' like a rifle-sling
  be'ind.

  While it's best foot first, etc.

At half-past five's Revelly, an' our tents they down
  must come,

Like a lot of button mushrooms when you pick 'em
  up at 'ome.

But it's over in a minute, an' at six the column starts,

While the women and the kiddies sit an' shiver in
  the carts.

  And it's best foot first, etc.

Oh, then it's open order, an' we lights our pipes an'
  sings,

An' we talks about our rations an' a lot of other
  things,

And we thinks o' friends in England, an' we wonders
  what they're at,

An' 'ow they would admire for to hear us sling
  the *bat*.[1]

  An' it's best foot first, etc.

[1]Thomas's first and firmest conviction is that he is a profound Orientalist and a fluent speaker of Hindustani. As a matter of fact, he depends largely on the sign-language.

It's none so bad o' Sunday, when you're lyin' at
    your ease,
To watch the kites a-wheelin' round them feather-
    'eaded trees,
For although there ain't no women, yet there ain't
    no barrick-yards,
So the orficers goes shootin' an' the men they plays
    at cards.
        Till it's best foot first, etc.

So 'ark an' 'eed you rookies, which is always grum-
    blin' sore,
There's worser things than marchin' from Umballa
    to Cawnpore;
And if your 'eels are blistered an' they feels to 'urt
    like 'ell
You drop some tallow in your socks an' that will
    make 'em well.
        For it's best foot first, etc.

We're marchin' on relief over Injia's coral strand,
Eight 'undred fightin' Englishmen, the Colonel. *and*
    the Band.

Ho! get away, you bullock-man, you've 'eard the
    bugle blowed,
There's a regiment a-comin' down the Grand Trunk
    Road.
        With its best foot first
        And the road a-sliding past,
        An' every bloomin' campin'-ground exactly
            like the last;
        While the Big Drum says,
        With 'is *"rowdy-dowdy-dow"*—
    "Kiko kissywarsti don't you *hamsher argyjow?"*[1]

                [1] Why don't you get on?

SHILLIN' A DAY

My name is O'Kelly, I've heard the Revelly
From Birr to Bareilly, from Leeds to Lahore,
Hong-Kong and Peshawur,
Lucknow and Etawah,
And fifty-five more all endin' in "pore."
Black Death and his quickness, the depth and the
    thickness,
Of sorrow and sickness I've known on my way,
But I'm old and I'm nervis,
I'm cast from the Service,
And all I deserve is a shillin' a day.

    (*Chorus.*)   Shillin' a day
                Bloomin' good pay —
                Lucky to touch it, a shillin' a day!

Oh, it drives me half crazy to think of the days I
Went slap for the Ghazi my sword at my side,

When we rode Hell-for-leather
Both squadrons together,
That didn't care whether we lived or we died.
But it's no use desparin', my wife must go charin'
An' me commissairin' the pay-bills to better,
So if me you be'old
In the wet and the cold,
By the Grand Metropold won't you give me a letter?
(*Full Chorus.*)   Give 'im a letter —
                Can't do no better
                Late Troop-Sergeant Major an'—
                    runs with a letter!
                Think what 'e's been,
                Think what 'e's seen,
                Think of his pensions an'——
                GAWD SAVE THE QUEEN!

L'ENVOI

THERE'S a whisper down the field where the year
 has shot her yield,
 And the ricks stand grey to the sun,
Singing:— "Over then, come over, for the bee has
 quit the clover,
 And your English summer's done."
  You have heard the beat of the off-shore wind,
  And the thresh of the deep-sea rain;
  You have heard the song — how long! how
   long?
  Pull out on the trail again!

  Ha' done with the Tents of Shem, dear lass,
  We've seen the seasons through,
  And it's time to turn on the old trail, our own
   trail, the out trail,
  Pull out, pull out, on the Long Trail — the
   trail that is always new.

It's North you may run to the rime-ringed sun
   Or South to the blind Horn's hate;
Or East all the way into Mississippi Bay,
   Or West to the Golden Gate;

      Where the blindest bluffs hold good, dear lass.
      And the wildest tales are true,
      And the men bulk big on the old trail, our own
         trail, the out trail,
      And life runs large on the Long Trail — the
         trail that is always new.

The days are sick and cold, and the skies are grey
    and old,
   And the twice-breathed airs blow damp;
And I'd sell my tired soul for the bucking beam-sea
    roll
   Of a black Bilbao tramp;

      With her load-line over her hatch, dear lass,
      And a drunken Dago crew,
      And her nose held down on the old trail, our
         own trail, the out trail
      From Cadiz Bar on the Long Trail — the
         trail that is always new.

There be triple ways to take, of the eagle or the snake,
  Or the way of a man with a maid;
But the sweetest way to me is a ship's upon the sea
  In the heel of the North-East Trade.

    Can you hear the crash on her bows, dear lass,
    And the drum of the racing screw,
    As she ships it green on the old trail, our own
        trail, the out trail,
    As she lifts and 'scends on the Long Trail — the
        trail that is always new?

See the shaking funnels roar, with the Peter at the
    fore,
  And the fenders grind and heave,
And the derricks clack and grate as the tackle
    hooks the crate,
  And the fall-rope whines through the sheave;

  It's "Gang-plank up and in," dear lass,
    It's "Hawsers warp her through!"
  And it's "All clear aft" on the old trail, our
      own trail, the out trail,
  We're backing down on the Long Trail — the
      trail that is always new.

Oh, the mutter overside, when the port-fog holds us
    tied,
  And the syrens hoot their dread!
When foot by foot we creep o'er the hueless viewless
    deep
    To the sob of the questing lead!
      It's down by the Lower Hope, dear lass,
      With the Gunfleet Sands in view,
      Till the Mouse swings green on the old trail,
        our own trail, the out trail,
      And the Gull Light lifts on the Long Trail —
        the trail that is always new.

Oh, the blazing tropic night, when the wake's a
    welt of light
  That holds the hot sky tame,
And the steady fore-foot snores through the planet-
    powdered floors
  Where the scared whale flukes in flame!
      Her plates are scarred by the sun, dear lass,
      Her ropes are taunt with the dew,
      For we're booming down on the old trail, our
        own trail, the out trail,
      We're sagging south on the Long Trail — the
        trail that is always new.

Then home, get her home where the drunken rollers
        comb,
   And the shouting seas drive by,
And the engines stamp and ring and the wet bows
        reel and swing,
   And the Southern Cross rides high!

      Yes, the old lost stars wheel back, dear lass,
      That blaze in the velvet blue.
      They're all old friends on the old trail, our
         own trail, the out trail,
      They're God's own guides on the Long Trail —
         the trail that is always new.

Fly forward, O my heart, from the Foreland to the
        Start —
   We're steaming all too slow,
And it's twenty thousand miles to our little lazy isle
   Where the trumpet-orchids blow!

      You have heard the call of the off-shore wind
      And the voice of the deep-sea rain —
      You have heard the song — how long! how
         long?
      Pull out on the trail again!

The Lord knows what we may find, dear lass,
And the Deuce knows what we may do —
But we're back once more on the old trail, our
    own trail, the out trail,
We're down, hull-down on the Long Trail —
    the trail that is always new.

THE COUNTRY LIFE PRESS
GARDEN CITY, N. Y.